second edition

BASIC GRAMMAR AND USAGE

Penelope Choy
Los Angeles City College

James McCormick
San Bernardino Valley College

HARCOURT BRACE JOVANOVICH, PUBLISHERS

San Diego   New York   Chicago   Atlanta   Washington, D.C.
London   Sydney   Toronto

ISBN: 0-15-504930-5

Library of Congress Catalog Card Number: 83-080018

Printed in the United States of America

Preface

The Second Edition of *Basic Grammar and Usage* retains the format of the First and Alternate Editions but incorporates revisions suggested by instructors who have used the earlier versions of this book.

The sequence of units has been changed so that the unit on Compound and Complex Sentences Versus Run-On Sentences and Fragments is treated earlier in the text. The lesson on Avoiding Fragments has been expanded. The Pronoun Usage unit now includes a discussion of ways to avoid sexist language. A new lesson on irregular verbs, including a list of some of the most commonly used irregular verbs, has been added to the text.

Because many instructors have asked for additional exercises, nearly all of the lessons now include three, rather than two, end-of-the-chapter exercises in addition to the numerous practice sentences contained within each lesson. The "A" exercises are intended primarily for in-class discussion, and the "B" exercises may be assigned as homework. The new "C" exercises are designed mainly to encourage production of sentences by the students in order to provide a bridge between the study of grammar and the writing of compositions. The Instructor's Manual has new pre-tests, unit tests, and achievement tests.

All of the exercises for this edition were written by James McCormick. The lessons for this edition and the tests in the Instructor's Manual were written by Penelope Choy.

The authors are grateful to the following instructors, who reviewed the previous editions of *Basic Grammar and Usage* and who suggested revisions for this edition:

Helen Quinn, University of Wisconsin-Stout; Suzanne Webb, Texas Woman's University; Patrick Seeley, Erie Community College; and Leo Dangel, Southwest State University.

The authors would also like to thank the people at Harcourt Brace Jovanovich who participated in the publication of this book: Bill McLane, senior editor, who initiated the plans for this edition; Marlane Agriesti, associate editor, who coordinated the writing and production of the book; Irene Pavitt, the manuscript editor; Mary-Ann Courtenaye, the production editor; Melinda Benson, the designer; and Lynn Edwards, the production manager.

Penelope Choy would like to thank everyone whose help during the past two years has made it possible for her to continue teaching and writing; in particular, her neurologist, Dr. Gregory O. Walsh, her colleagues at Los Angeles City College, and the members of her myasthenia gravis support group.

James McCormick would like to thank Sharon Swann, who typed his portion of the manuscript, and Virginia, who endured.

Penelope Choy
James McCormick

Preface to the First Edition

Basic Grammar and Usage was originally written for students in a special admissions program at the University of California, Los Angeles. As part of their participation in the program, the students were enrolled in a composition and grammar course designed to prepare them for the university's freshman English courses. When the program began in 1971, none of the grammar textbooks then on the market seemed suitable for the students, whose previous exposure to grammar had been cursory or, in some cases, nonexistent. As the director of the program's English classes, I decided to write a book of my own that would cover the most important areas of grammar and usage in a way that would be easily understood by my students.

The original version of *Basic Grammar and Usage* received an enthusiastic response from the students and was used successfully throughout the three-year duration of the program. After the program ended in 1974, many of the instructors asked permission to reproduce the book for use in their new teaching positions. By the time copies of *Basic Grammar and Usage* reached Harcourt Brace Jovanovich in 1975, the text had already been used by more than 1,500 students in nearly a dozen schools.

Basic Grammar and Usage presents material in small segments so that students can master a particular topic one step at a time. The lessons within each unit are cumulative. For example, students doing the pronoun exercises for Lesson 19 will find that those exercises include a review of the constructions treated in Lessons 16 to 18. This approach reinforces the students' grasp of the material and helps them develop the skills they need for the writing of compositions. To make them more interesting to students, the exercises in four of the six units are presented as short narratives rather than as lists of unrelated sentences. Each lesson concludes with two exercises, which may be either used in class or assigned as homework. In addition, each unit ends with a composition that the students must proofread for errors and then correct to demonstrate mastery of the material.

Students who have never before studied grammar systematically will find that working through the text from beginning to end provides an insight into the basic patterns of English grammar. As one student commented on an end-of-course evaluation, "The most important thing I learned from *Basic Grammar and Usage* is that if you learn what an independent clause is, half of your grammar problems are over." On the other hand, students who do not need a total review of grammar can concentrate on the specific areas in which they have weaknesses. To help the instructor evaluate both types of student, the Instructor's Manual accompanying the text includes a diagnostic test and a post-test divided into sections corresponding to the units in the book. There are also separate achievement tests for each unit, as well as answer keys to the exercises presented in the text.

Although *Basic Grammar and Usage* is designed for students whose native language is English, it has been used successfully by students learning English as a second language. In addition to being a classroom text, *Basic Grammar and Usage* can be used in writing labs and for individual tutoring.

Many people have shared in the preparation of *Basic Grammar and Usage*. I wish in particular to thank the instructors and administrators of UCLA's Academic Advancement Program, where this book originated. In revising the text for publication, I have been greatly helped by the suggestions of Regina Sackmary of Queensborough Community College of the City University of New York and by Elizabeth Gavin, formerly of California State University, Long Beach, who reviewed the manuscript for me. Sue Houchins of the Black Studies Center of the Claremont Colleges contributed many ideas and reference materials for the exercises. An author could not ask for more supportive people to work with than the staff of Harcourt Brace Jovanovich. I owe a special debt of gratitude to Raoul Savoie, who first brought the UCLA version of the text to the attention of his company. I also wish to thank Lauren Procton, who was responsible for the editing, and Eben W. Ludlow, who has provided guidance and encouragement throughout all the stages of this book's development.

Penelope Choy

Table of Contents

Identifying Subjects and Verbs

1 **Sentences with One Subject and One Verb**

The most important grammatical skill you can learn is how to identify subjects and verbs. Just as solving arithmetic problems requires you to know the multiplication tables perfectly, solving grammatical problems requires you to identify subjects and verbs with perfect accuracy. This is not as difficult as it sounds. With practice, recognizing subjects and verbs will become as automatic as knowing that $2 \times 2 = 4$.

Although in conversation people often speak in short word groups that may not be complete sentences, in written English people usually use complete sentences.

A complete sentence contains at least one subject and one verb.

A sentence can be thought of as a statement describing an *actor* performing a particular *action*. For example, in the sentence "The man fell," the *actor* or person performing the action is the *man*. What *action* did the man perform? He *fell*. This *actor–action* pattern can be found in most sentences. Can you identify the actor and the action in each of the sentences below?

The band played.
The woman coughed.

The *actor* in a sentence is called the **subject.** The *action* word in a sentence is called the **verb.** Together, the subject and verb form the core of the sentence. Notice that even if extra words are added to the two sentences above, the subject—verb core in each sentence remains the same.

The *band played* John Philip Sousa's "Stars and Stripes Forever."
The *woman* in the row behind me *coughed* during the entire movie.

You can see that in order to identify subjects and verbs, you must be able to separate these core words from the rest of the words in the sentence.

Here are some suggestions to help you identify verbs.

1. The *action* words in sentences are verbs. For example:

The audience *applauded*.
I *drive* thirty miles each day.
My daughter *hates* spinach.

Underline the verb in each of the following sentences.

The bank opens at ten o'clock.

The landlord painted my apartment.

We ate a pizza for lunch.

2. All forms of the verb *be* are verbs: *am, is, are, was, were,* and *been.* For example:

Sam *is* unhappy.
The athletes *were* very healthy.

Verbs also include words that can be used as substitutes for forms of *be,* such as *seem, feel, become,* and *appear.* These verbs are called **linking verbs**.

Sam *feels* unhappy.
The athletes *seemed* very healthy.

Underline the verb in each of the following sentences.

I am nervous about my new job.

Wayne becomes nervous during tests.

The witness appeared nervous during the trial.

3. Verbs are the only words that change their spelling to show tense. **Tense** is the time—present, past, or future—at which the verb's action occurs. For example, the sentence "We *work* for United Airlines" has a present-tense verb. The sentence "We *worked* for United Airlines" has a past-tense verb. Underline the verb in each of the following sentences.

I enjoy hot fudge sundaes.

Linda enjoyed last night's party.

The club meets once a week.

Tom met me at the bus stop.

The children need new shoes.

The town needed a new high school.

Identifying verbs will be easier for you if you remember that the following kinds of words are *not* verbs.

4. An **infinitive**—the combination of the word *to* plus a verb, such as *to walk* or *to study*—is *not* considered part of the verb in a sentence. Read the following sentences.

The doctor wants to see you.
The mechanic tried to fix my car.

The verbs in these two sentences are *wants* and *tried*. The infinitives *to see* and *to fix* are *not* included. Underline the verb in each of the following sentences. Do *not* include infinitives.

The team expects to win the game.

My friend plans to buy a new car.

5. **Adverbs**—words that describe a verb—are *not* part of the verb. Many commonly used adverbs end in *-ly*. The adverbs in the following sentences are italicized. Underline the verb in each sentence.

The sportscaster spoke *rapidly*.

The burglar entered the house *quietly*.

The baby cried *loudly*.

The words *not, never,* and *very* are also adverbs. Like other adverbs, these words are *not* part of the verb. Underline the verb in each of the following sentences. Do *not* include adverbs.

My parents never forget my birthday.

Susan smiled happily.

I quickly prepared dinner.

The professor is not here today.

The nurse carefully examined the patient.

This factory operates very efficiently.

Now that you can identify verbs, here are some suggestions to help you to identify subjects.

1. The subject of a sentence is most frequently a noun. A **noun** is the name of a person, place, or thing, such as *Laura, Dallas,* or *pencils.* A noun may also be the name of an abstract idea, such as *happiness* or *success.* Underline the subject in each of the following sentences *once* and the verb *twice.* Remember that the verb is the *action,* and the subject is the *actor.*

Susan works two days a week.

The plane arrived on time.

Arizona contains many Indian reservations.

Jealousy destroyed their marriage.

2. The subject of a sentence may also be a **subject pronoun. A pronoun** is a word used in place of a noun, such as *she (= Laura), it (= Dallas),* or *they (= pencils).* The following words are subject pronouns:

I, you, he, she, it, we, they

Underline the subject in each of the following sentences *once* and the verb *twice*.

He lost his wallet.

It rained yesterday.

Last month I earned two thousand dollars.

They bought a new car.

3. In **commands,** such as "Shut the door!", the subject is understood to be the subject pronoun *you,* even though the word *you* is almost never included in the command. *You* is understood to be the subject of the following sentences.

Call an ambulance!
Please turn off your radio.

Underline the subject in each of the following sentences *once* and the verb *twice.* If the sentence is a command, write the subject *you* in parentheses at the beginning of the sentence.

The water flooded the streets.

Listen to me.

He borrowed my car.

Please help me with the dishes.

Identifying subjects will be easier for you if you remember that the following kinds of words are *not* subjects.

4. **Adjectives**—words that describe a noun—are *not* part of the subject. For example, in the sentence "The young actress won an Oscar," the subject is "actress," *not* "young actress." In the sentence "A private college charges tuition," the subject is "college," *not* "private college." Underline the subject in each of the following sentences *once* and the verb *twice*.

The new theater opens tomorrow.

A police officer arrested the thief.

Chocolate chip cookies are my favorite dessert. (Notice that more than one

   adjective may precede — come before — the subject of a sentence.)

A large brown dog bit me.

5. Words that show **possession,** or ownership, are *not* part of the subject. Words that show possession include nouns ending in an apostrophe (') combined with *s,* such as *David's* or *car's*. They also include **possessive pronouns,** words that replace nouns showing ownership, such as *his (= David's)* or *its (= car's)*. Possessive pronouns include the following words:

   my, your, his, her, its, our, their

Since words that show possession are *not* part of the subject, in the sentence "My daughter wears glasses," the subject is "daughter," *not* "my daughter." In the sentence "Judy's landlord raised the rent," the subject is "landlord," *not* "Judy's landlord." Underline the subject in each of the following sentences *once* and the verb *twice*.

Tim's son waxed the car.

Our house has three bedrooms.

California's largest industry is agriculture.

My neighbor's dog barked all night long.

Here is a final suggestion to help you to identify subjects and verbs accurately.

Try to identify the verb in a sentence before you try to identify the subject.

A sentence may have many nouns, any of which could be the subject, but it will usually have only one or two verbs. For example:

The theater in my neighborhood offers a special discount to students and senior citizens.

There are five nouns in the above sentence *(theater, neighborhood, discount, students, citizens),* any of which might be the subject. However, there is only one verb — *offers.* Once you have identified the verb as *offers,* all you have to ask yourself is, "Who or what offers?" The answer is *theater,* which is the subject of the sentence.

Identify the subject and verb in the following sentence, remembering to look for the verb first.

The captain of my high-school football team now plays for the Pittsburgh

Steelers.

Remember these basic points:

1. The action being performed in a sentence is the **verb.**
2. The person or thing performing the action is the **subject.**
3. A sentence consists of an *actor* performing an *action,* or, in other words, a **subject** plus a **verb.**

Since every sentence you write will have a subject and a verb, you must be able to identify subjects and verbs in order to write correctly. Therefore, as you do the exercises in this unit, apply the rules you have learned in each lesson, and *think* about what you are doing. Do not make random guesses. Grammar is based on logic, not on luck.

Underline the subject in each of the following sentences *once* and the verb *twice.* Add the subject *you* in parentheses if the sentence is a command.

We missed last night's football game.

The witness refused to answer any questions.

Fresh fish spoils rapidly.

His wallet contains only two dollars.

Drive carefully.

The recipe's ingredients are very expensive.

She is not here.

EXERCISE 1A

Underline the subject of each sentence *once* and the verb *twice*. Each sentence has one subject and one verb. *Remember to look for the verb first* before you try to locate the subject.

1. Children everywhere acquire language in a similar pattern.

2. This natural pattern begins with the basic elements of grammar.

3. A child's first words are usually nouns like *Mama*.

4. Some children begin with verbs like *go* or *want*.

5. A child's first sentences have only a few words.

6. "I want Mama."

7. Even these short sentences show the child's sense of grammatical structure.

8. Some children learn very quickly to make commands.

9. "Give me juice!"

10. The average three-year-old child has a vocabulary of 800 to 900 words.

11. His or her sentences are often five to ten words long.

12. Children gradually learn to modify nouns with adjectives and to modify verbs with adverbs.

13. They form negative sentences with *not*.

14. Past-tense verbs become easier for them.

15. Many sentence combinations begin to appear in their conversations.

16. Of course, a child's grammatical abilities are unconscious and intuitive.

17. This book attempts to bring your unconscious sense of grammar to the surface.

18. It also starts with nouns and verbs.

19. All sentences (in every language) build from this foundation.

EXERCISE 1B

Underline the subject of each sentence *once* and the verb *twice*. Each sentence has one subject and one verb. *Remember to look for the verb first* before you try to locate the subject.

1. Some sentences have a sense of humor.

2. These sentences are little jokes.

3. Have fun with them.

4. The subject of this sentence is one word.

5. This sentence's subject contains no apostrophe.

6. This sentence's verb begins with the second letter of the alphabet.

7. The verb here is a linking verb.

8. Sometimes an adverb is the first word in a sentence.

9. Adverbs sometimes come just in front of the verb.

10. Try to find the infinitive in this command.

11. Adverbs usually end in *-ly*.

12. Some adverbs never end in *-ly*.

13. This exercise tries to sharpen your awareness of grammatical form.

14. Check each subject and verb again.

15. The human imagination likes to smile occasionally.

EXERCISE 1C

Each group of words below is missing *one* word to make it a complete sentence. The missing word may be a subject, or it may be a verb. Make each group of words into a sentence by adding *one* noun, *one* subject pronoun, or *one* verb.

1. Last week Jane _____ early.

2. _____ liked chocolate cake.

3. Yesterday _____ saw Bill Jones.

4. The _____ ran across the street.

5. The new _____ stopped too soon.

6. Last Christmas _____ visited relatives.

7. Her _____ wanted to be a U.S. Marine.

8. The boy's _____ was very happy.

9. It occasionally _____ during last winter.

10. _____ went there on the Fourth of July.

11. _____ your present!

12. The car's _____ never gave them any trouble.

13. The cool _____ was most pleasant.

14. My youngest uncle's _____ married a musician.

15. _____ the door gently.

16. His little green _____ was the favorite last month.

17. They _____ him this past year.

18. His bike's original paint _____ blue.

2 Multiple Subjects and Verbs

Some sentences have more than one subject. Others have more than one verb. Many sentences have more than one subject *and* more than one verb. The subjects in the following sentences have been labeled with an "S" and the verbs with a "V."

   S   V   V

I vacuumed the carpets and mopped the floors.

        S   S   V

My brother and his wife bought a new house.

         S   V   S   V

This restaurant serves good food, but its prices are expensive.

         S   V   S   V

Because Elaine speaks three languages, she got a job at the United Nations.

You can identify the pattern of a sentence by indicating how many subjects and verbs it has. Although in theory a sentence can have any number of subjects and verbs, the most common patterns are:

S-V   one subject and one verb
S-V-V   one subject and two verbs

S-S-V   two subjects and one verb
S-V/S-V   two subjects and two verbs

Underline the subjects of the following sentences *once* and the verbs *twice*.

The dentist examined my teeth.

He found a cavity and filled it.

The art teacher and his students visited the museum.

My operation cost twenty thousand dollars, but my insurance paid the bill.

Any group of words that contains *at least one subject and one verb* is called a **clause.** Therefore, any sentence with one S-V, S-V-V, or S-S-V pattern contains one clause. Sentences that contain only one clause are called **simple sentences.**

Sentences that contain more than one clause (each with its own subject and verb) are known as either **compound** or **complex sentences,** depending upon the kind of word that is used to join the clauses. You will study compound and complex sentences in detail in later lessons, but at the present time the important thing for you to learn is how to identify *all* the subjects and verbs in a sentence that has more than one clause.

The clauses in compound and complex sentences are joined by words called **conjunctions.** A conjunction (from a Latin word meaning ''to join together'') is a word that joins words or groups of words — such as the clauses you are now studying. The following conjunctions are used to join clauses in **compound sentences:**

and   but   for   nor   or   so   yet

A compound sentence must have at least *two* subjects and *two* verbs, usually arranged in an S-V/S-V pattern. The conjunction comes in the middle of the two clauses. For example:

        S   V   S   V
The professor lectured, *and* the students took notes.

S V   S   V
I phoned you last night, *but* you were not home.

Underline *all* the subjects of the following compound sentences *once* and *all* the verbs *twice*.

We have a test tomorrow, and I need to study.

My neighbor wants to remodel her apartment, but her lease prohibits it.

Larry stayed home, for his daughter was ill.

You pay your bills on time, or you ruin your credit rating.

Susan is not here, nor is Sarah. (When the clauses in a compound sentence

are joined by *nor,* the pattern becomes S-V/V-S.)

Barry had no cash, so he used a credit card.

The team fumbled the ball five times, yet they won the game.

Are you remembering to look for the verb in each clause first?

There are several types of **complex sentences,** and each type uses different conjunctions. The conjunctions that are used in the following sentences describe *time, place, reason,* and *condition.*

$$\text{\quad\quad\quad\ S\quad\ V\quad\quad S\quad\ V}$$
When the game ended, the fans cheered.

$$\text{\quad\quad S\quad\ V\quad\quad\quad\quad\quad\quad S\quad V}$$
The patient carries his medicine *wherever* he goes.

$$\text{S\quad\ V\quad\quad\quad\ S\quad\ V}$$
We moved *because* we needed a bigger house.

$$\text{\quad\quad\ S\quad\ V\quad\quad\ S\quad\quad\ V}$$
If the witness lied, the defendant deserves a new trial.

Some of the conjunctions used in the type of complex sentence discussed in this lesson are:

time after, as, before, until, when, whenever, while
place where, wherever
reason because, since, so that (*not* ''so'')
condition although, even though, if, unless

Notice that the conjunction may come before the first clause, as in:

$$\text{\quad\quad\quad\ S\quad\ V\quad\ S\quad\ V}$$
When my boss retired, he moved to Hawaii.

Or it may come before the second clause:

       S   V   S   V
Babies cry *when* they are hungry.

Underline *all* the subjects of the following complex sentences *once* and *all* the verbs *twice*. Also circle the conjunction in each sentence. Notice that each sentence contains at least *two* subjects and *two* verbs in an S-V/S-V pattern.

Because I like ravioli, I often eat at Italian restaurants.

The professor explained the lesson while the students listened.

He does his homework whenever he has the time.

Even though large automobiles use a lot of gas, people still buy them.

EXERCISE 2A

Underline the subjects of the following sentences *once* and the verbs *twice*. Remember not to include infinitives as part of the verb. To help you, the pattern of each sentence is indicated in parentheses.

1. *West Side Story* is a powerful musical drama of love and revenge. (S-V)

2. The Jets gang plans to challenge the Sharks gang to a street fight at an upcoming dance. (S-V)

3. Bernardo leads the Sharks, and Riff leads the Jets. (S-V/S-V)

4. Riff persuades his old friend Tony to help him at the dance. (S-V)

5. There Tony meets the beautiful Maria, but she is Bernardo's sister. (S-V/S-V)

6. At first sight, Tony and Maria fall in love. (S-S-V)

7. The two gangs agree to a fight between Bernardo and Riff, with no weapons. (S-V)

8. Bernardo is furious because Maria loves Tony instead of his buddy Chino. (S-V/S-V)

9. Suddenly, Bernardo pulls a knife and kills Riff. (S-V-V)

10. Tony grabs the knife, and he stabs Bernardo to death. (S-V/S-V)

11. The gangs rush at each other to fight but run away at the sound of the police. (S-V-V)

12. When Maria learns about the Sharks's plans to kill Tony, she sends Anita to warn him. (S-V/S-V)

13. But the Jets assault Anita because she was Bernardo's girl. (S-V/S-V)

14. To get even, she tells them that Chino killed Maria. (S-V/S-V)

15. Tony hears this false report and comes out of hiding. (S-V-V)

16. He wanders the streets and finds Maria. (S-V-V)

17. Suddenly Chino appears, shoots Tony, and kills him. (S-V-V-V)

18. As Maria kneels beside Tony, the gangs assemble and declare a truce. (S-V/S-V-V)

19. Then they carry Tony away, and the curtain falls. (S-V/S-V)

20. Shakespeare told a similar story long ago, but he called it *Romeo and Juliet*. (S-V/S-V)

EXERCISE 2B

Underline the subjects of the following sentences *once* and the verbs *twice*. Some sentences have more than one subject, more than one verb, or both.

1. This story illustrates the attitude of the Navaho Indian toward hardship.

2. Two cowboys wanted to travel across a long stretch of desert, so they hired a Navaho to guide them.

3. The three men filled their canteens, put food in their saddlebags, and began their trip.

4. At night they camped and cooked their food.

5. The Indian talked very little, but he always ate his share of the food.

6. During the fifth night, a sudden storm broke, and the frightened horses ran away with the saddlebags of food.

7. With only their canteens, the three men began the long walk toward a town.

8. The two cowboys talked endlessly about food, but the Navaho said nothing.

9. The cowboys remembered delicious steaks, and they planned enormous dinners in their imaginations.

10. But whenever they asked the Indian about food, he always said, "Not me."

11. At last they reached a town.

12. The three men ate a huge meal of steak, beans, bread, and coffee.

13. Finally the cowboys were full, but the Navaho ate and ate and ate.

14. The cowboys were amazed, so one cowboy spoke to the Indian.

15. "You said 'Not me' back in the desert, but now you eat enough for six men!"

16. The Navaho answered, "We had no food back in the desert."

EXERCISE 2C

The following sentences need more than one subject, more than one verb, or both. Put *one* noun, *one* subject pronoun, or *one* verb in each blank to complete each sentence.

1. Mary and _____ became good friends.

2. The _____ and the _____

   sat in the parking lot.

3. Yesterday the girl _____ and

   _____ her car.

4. In 1981 my _____ and I repaired and

   _____ an old truck.

5. Her _____ and her _____

   painted the apartment.

6. At the last homecoming the band _____ on the

   field, _____ for the signal, and

   _____ to play the school song.

7. After he _____ last night, she

   _____ this morning.

8. My uncle _____ in bed last week because he

   _____ a bad cold.

9. His former boss _____, so he

_____.

10. _____ left the party early, and

_____ never returned.

11. _____, _____, and

_____ seemed to be together all the time.

12. _____ your book and then

_____ it.

13. Tom and _____ sat beside each other in high

school but _____ to different colleges last

September.

14. The _____ in the car waved to his friend just as

the car _____ into the lamppost.

15. The _____ shouted at the woman after she

_____ and _____.

3 Distinguishing Between Objects of Prepositions and Subjects

One of the most common causes of errors in identifying the subject of a sentence is confusing it with a noun used as the object of a preposition. To avoid making this type of mistake, you first must learn to recognize prepositions and prepositional phrases.

Prepositions are the short words in our language that show the *position* of one object in relation to another. For example, if you were trying to describe where a particular book was located, you might say:

The book is *on* the desk.
The book is *in* the drawer.
The book is *by* the table.
The book is *under* the notebook.
The book is *behind* him.

The italicized words are all prepositions. They show the position of the book in relation to the desk, the drawer, the notebook, and him.

Here is a list of the most common prepositions. You do not have to memorize these words, but you must be able to recognize them as prepositions when you see them.

about	beside	of
above	between	on
across	by	onto
after	concerning	over
against	down	through
along	during	to
amid	except	toward
among	for	under
around	from	up
at	in	upon
behind	into	with
below	like	within
beneath	near	without

As you can see from the sentences describing the location of the book, prepositions are not used by themselves; they are always placed in front of a noun or pronoun. The noun or pronoun following the preposition is called the **object of the preposition.** The group of words containing the preposition and its object is called a **prepositional phrase.** Any words, such as adjectives or the words *a, an,* or *the,* which come between the preposition and its object are also part of the prepositional phrase. Read the following sentences, in which the prepositional phrases are italicized. Notice that each prepositional phrase begins with a preposition and ends with a noun or pronoun.

I keep my keys *in my purse.*
The restaurant is *across the street.*
The bride stood *beside the groom.*
A bowl *of soup* costs seventy-five cents.
Jean eats lunch *with me.*

Some prepositional phrases may have more than one object.

The bank closes *on weekends and holidays.*
I like pizza *with pepperoni and anchovies.*

It is also possible to have two or more prepositional phrases in a row.

We sat *in the shade of a large tree.*
The driver *in the car in front of me* suddenly changed lanes.

Circle the prepositional phrases in the following sentences. Some sentences may have more than one prepositional phrase.

The wind blew against my face.

He went to the party without me.

A bridge connects the cities of San Francisco and Oakland.

The child was lost amid the crowd of shoppers.

Construct sentences of your own containing prepositional phrases. Use the prepositions listed below. Make certain that each of your sentences contains at least one subject and one verb.

with: _____

_____

through: _____

_____

by: _____

_____

of: _____

_____

at: _____

_____

The words *before* and *after* may be used either as prepositions or as conjunctions (p. 17). If the word is being used as a preposition, it will be followed by a noun or pronoun object. If the word is being used as a conjunction, it will be followed by both a subject and a verb.

As a Preposition	*As a Conjunction*
The movie ended *before midnight*.	S V *Before* he does his homework, he eats a little snack.

He retired *after his*   We left the restaurant *after* we finished dinner.
seventieth birthday.

What do prepositional phrases have to do with identifying subjects and verbs? The answer is simple.

Any word that is part of a prepositional phrase cannot be the subject or the verb of a sentence.

This rule works for two reasons:

Any noun or pronoun in a prepositional phrase must be the object of the preposition, and the object of a preposition cannot also be a subject.
and
Prepositional phrases never contain verbs.

To see how this rule can help you to identify subjects and verbs, read the following twenty-four-word sentence:

During my flight to Hawaii, the passenger in the seat beside me knocked a glass of orange juice from his tray onto my lap.

If you want to find the subject and verb of this sentence, you know that they will not be part of any of the sentence's prepositional phrases. So, cross out all the prepositional phrases in the sentence.

~~During my flight to Hawaii~~, the passenger ~~in the seat beside me~~ knocked a glass ~~of orange juice from his tray onto my lap.~~

You now have only five words left out of the original twenty-four, and you know that the subject and verb must be within these five words. What are the subject and verb?

Read the following sentence, and cross out all of its prepositional phrases.

At night the lights from the oil refinery glow in the dark.

If you crossed out all the prepositional phrases, you should be left with only three words — *the lights glow.* Which word is the subject, and which is the verb?

Identify the subject and verb in the following sentence. Cross out the prepositional phrases first.

In the summer, both of the children go to their grandmother's house for two

weeks.

If you identified all of the prepositional phrases, you should be left with only two words — the subject *both* and the verb *go*.

Now you can see another reason why it is important to be able to identify prepositional phrases. It might *seem* logical for the subject of the sentence to be *children*. However, since *of the children* is a prepositional phrase, *children* cannot be the subject. Instead, the subject is *both*.

Underline the subjects of the following sentences *once* and the verbs *twice*. Remember to cross out prepositional phrases first.

The main highway from Arizona to California runs through the Mojave

Desert.

All of the tellers in the bank are responsible for their own cash drawers.

An elderly woman with five cats lives in the apartment above me.

A line of cars extended for three miles along the freeway from the site of

the accident.

His collection of paintings includes works by famous American artists like

Winslow Homer and Georgia O'Keeffe.

Underline the subjects of the following compound and complex sentences *once* and the verbs *twice*. Remember that each sentence will have at least two subjects and two verbs. Cross out prepositional phrases first.

When one of the babies in the nursery starts to cry, all of the other babies

cry too.

The aroma of Italian food drifted out of the restaurant, and people on the

sidewalk stopped to look at the menu in the window.

EXERCISE 3A

Underline the subjects of the following sentences *once* and the verbs *twice*. Some sentences may have more than one subject, more than one verb, or both. Remember to cross out the prepositional phrases first.

1. No other state in the United States has the unusual geology of Hawaii.

2. The tips of a chain of submerged volcanic peaks form the Hawaiian Islands.

3. The entire chain of islands and atolls stretches over 1500 miles across the central Pacific Ocean.

4. People live on the eight major islands at the eastern end of the chain.

5. From west to east they are the islands of Niihau, Kauai, Oahu, Molokai, Lanai, Kahoolawe, Maui, and Hawaii.

6. The islands to the east are younger because their formation came last.

7. Only the easternmost and largest island of Hawaii is still volcanically active.

8. That island's craters of Mauna Loa and Kilauea occasionally erupt with spectacular lava flows, and a lava fountain from Kilauea shot 1900 feet into the air in 1959.

9. The many high ridges of the islands combine with moist trade winds to bring almost daily rain to most places in the islands.

10. In fact, the nearly 600 inches of rain per year on Kauai's highest peak makes it the rainiest place on earth.

11. However, some parts of the islands were almost totally dry until engineers discovered huge natural reservoirs of fresh water within the islands' porous volcanic formations.

12. Now even the dry areas of Hawaii have fresh water from wells in these great underground reserves.

13. Sometimes it pays to live on a volcano.

EXERCISE 3B

Underline the subjects of the following sentences *once* and the verbs *twice*. Some sentences may have more than one subject, more than one verb, or both. Remember to cross out the prepositional phrases first.

1. Most blind people use the same system to keep track of their money.

2. They memorize the feel of coins by size and shape.

3. The dollar is the largest and heaviest coin.

4. Its rim has many small notches, or *serrations*.

5. The second largest coin is the half dollar.

6. The quarter comes next.

7. Both of these coins also have edges with serrations.

8. The nickel is next in size.

9. Its rim is smooth and free of any notches.

10. The penny also has a smooth rim, is slightly smaller than the nickel, and weighs much less.

11. The smallest coin of all is the dime.

12. It weighs very little and has a rim with extremely fine serrations.

13. To get the feeling of being blind, close your eyes and try to count a handful of change.

14. The uniform size of all paper money makes bills a greater problem than coins.

15. The blind person usually keeps his bills in the following manner.

16. The ones lie flat in the wallet.

17. Each of the fives gets one fold to give it almost a square shape.

18. The tens get one fold lengthwise.

19. The twenties get two folds lengthwise for a very long narrow shape.

20. Blind people usually carry no twos or very large bills like fifties.

21. Fortunately, only a small percentage of clerks short-change their blind customers.

22. Disabled people need to feel independent, so the blind learn to see with their hands.

EXERCISE 3C

A prepositional phrase adds more meaning to a sentence, but it also adds a noun or a pronoun that may be mistaken for the subject. Add a prepositional phrase to each of the following sentences. Then underline the subject of the sentence *once* and the verb *twice*. The first sentence has been done as an example.

in the green dress
1. The <u>girl</u> ∧ <u><u>left</u></u> early.

2. The car was crashed.

3. That girl is new.

4. The boss hired three new people.

5. That location is a good one.

6. The group sat alone.

7. Her knowledge amazes everyone.

8. The top is too high.

9. Open the box.

10. The amount surprised the collector.

A preposition is always followed by its object, though it may not be the very next word. In each of the following sentences a preposition is missing its object. Put in a noun or a pronoun for the missing object. Then underline the subject of the sentence *once* and the verb *twice*. The first sentence has been done as an example.

girls
11. <u>Each</u> of the ∧ <u><u>won</u></u> a prize.

12. A glass of costs a quarter.

13. In the he leaves for work.

14. Some players on the got sick.

15. All of the remain here on Friday.

16. During the, the house fell down.

17. Many people go to the in the summer.

18. A tank of costs more in some places.

19. At the his brother won a medal.

20. One of the women smiled with.

4 Main Verbs and Helping Verbs

Verbs can be either **main verbs** or **helping** (also called **auxiliary**) **verbs.** Main verbs are the kind of verb you have already studied. Main verbs tell what action is being performed in a sentence. For example:

I *quit* my job last week.
The fire *destroyed* three homes.

Helping verbs are used in combination with main verbs. They perform two major functions:

1. Helping verbs indicate shades of meaning that cannot be expressed by a main verb alone. Consider the differences in meaning in the following sentences, in which the helping verbs have been italicized.

    I *may* quit my job soon.
    I *must* quit my job soon.
    I *should* quit my job soon.
    I *can* quit my job soon.

As you can see, changing the helping verb changes the meaning of the entire sentence. These differences in meaning could not be expressed simply by using the main verb *quit* alone.

2. Helping verbs also show tense—the time at which the action of the verb takes place. Notice how changing the helping verb in the following sentences changes the tense of the main verb *watch*. (Both the helping and the main verbs have been italicized.)

The children *are watching* television now.
The children *will watch* television after dinner.
The children *have watched* television all evening.

Notice the position that helping verbs have in a sentence. They always *come before* the main verb, although sometimes another word, such as an adverb, may come between the helping verb and the main verb.

You *can answer* the question.
You *can* probably *answer* the question.
She *should save* more money.
She *should* definitely *save* more money.

If a question contains a helping verb, the helping verb still comes *before* the main verb.

Can you *answer* the question?
Should she *save* more money?
Does he *own* a car?
Where *are* you *going?*

The following words are helping verbs. *Memorize them.*

can, could
may, might, must
shall, should
will, would

The following words can be used either as helping verbs or as main verbs.

They are helping verbs if they are used in combination with a main verb. They are main verbs if they occur alone. *Memorize them.*

has, have, had   (forms of the verb *have*)
does, do, did, done   (forms of the verb *do*)
am, is, are, was, were, been   (forms of the verb *be*)

As Main Verbs

I *have* a cold.
We *did* the laundry.
She *is* here now.

As Helping Verbs

I *have studied* French.
We *did* not *eat* breakfast.
She *is sleeping* now.

From now on, whenever you are asked to identify the verbs in a sentence, *include all the main verbs and all the helping verbs.* For example, in the sentence "We should review this lesson," the complete verb is "should review." In the sentence "He has lost his wallet," the verb is "has lost." Underline the complete verbs in the following sentences.

Steve must finish his term paper tonight.

Gail may move to Washington next year.

The team should win this game easily.

I was looking for a larger apartment.

Some sentences may contain more than one helping verb.

one helping verb   The landlord *will increase* our rent.
two helping verbs   The plane *should be arriving* soon.
three helping verbs   The new highway *must have been completed* by now.

Underline the subjects of the following sentences *once* and the complete verbs *twice*.

You should have paid your income tax on time.

Lena and Jay will be getting married in June.

He might not have seen me.

We have been waiting for you.

Do you know my new address?

Can you babysit for us tonight?

Remember this rule:

The verbs in a sentence include all the main verbs plus all the help-ing verbs.

EXERCISE 4A

Underline the subjects of the following sentences *once* and the complete verbs *twice*. Some sentences may have more than one subject, more than one set of verbs, or both. Remember to cross out prepositional phrases first.

1. In 1891 the leaders of the international YMCAs were faced with a problem.

2. Though YMCA memberships had been growing steadily, attendance in the winter months would drop sharply.

3. The leaders decided to strengthen their winter sports program with a new game.

4. They asked Dr. James Naismith to invent a fast indoor game for winter evenings.

5. After a study of outdoor team games, Dr. Naismith was convinced to use a large round ball for his new game.

6. To eliminate rough play, the ball would not be carried by the players.

7. Instead it would be passed from player to player, or it would be bounced on the floor.

8. Dr. Naismith did not want to have defensive players in a group around the goals.

9. So he placed the goals high in the air.

10. For the first trial of his new game, Dr. Naismith used two peach baskets as goals.

11. He put the baskets at the opposite ends of the YMCA gymnasium in Springfield, Massachusetts.

12. On that night the game of ''basketball'' was born.

13. The new game grew very rapidly in popularity.

14. Soon basketball was being played everywhere in the country.

15. In 1898 a professional basketball league was formed.

16. By 1906, the peach-basket goals had been replaced with metal hoops.

17. By 1913, 20 million people were playing the sport, and the rules were printed in thirty languages throughout the world.

18. Today basketball is enjoyed on every part of the globe by amateurs and professionals.

19. Since 1936, it has been a regular part of the Olympic Games.

20. For a long time the American team was considered the favorite to win every gold medal for Olympic basketball.

21. But since so many countries have adopted this fast-moving sport, the U.S. can no longer be sure of victory in the Olympics.

22. In less than one hundred years, Dr. Naismith's game with two peach baskets has become almost everyone's game.

EXERCISE 4B

Underline the subjects of the following sentence *once* and the complete verbs *twice*. Some sentences may have more than one subject, more than one set of verbs, or both. Remember to cross out prepositional phrases first.

1. I was watching the bright yellow float on my fishing line, but the float never moved.

2. On my hook a little minnow swam as bait three feet below the shining surface of the lake.

3. Bob and I had been fishing without luck for three hours on this beautiful November afternoon.

4. Because I had never fished for bass before, he had shown me how to bait the hook.

5. We had picked the very end of a long dock as the perfect spot.

6. No sound except our whispers broke the stillness, and the lake and trees were glowing gold in the last rays of the sun.

7. "Should we go now before it gets dark?"

8. Bob gave me a very puzzling answer.

9. "We must stay, for the moment of truth is coming!"

10. Before I could say another word, a great bass leaped straight up in front of us.

11. Then suddenly my yellow float was snatched under the water, and my fishing pole bent down in an arc.

12. I pulled in a big bass and baited my hook with another minnow.

13. As the minnow hit the water, it was grabbed by another fish.

14. I caught it, and then I caught another and another.

15. We fished like two crazy men until we had caught over thirty bass.

16. Suddenly it was dark, and the bass were gone.

17. As we walked home with our load of fish, I asked Bob to explain his prediction about our moment of truth.

18. "When I am fishing, I think like a fish!"

EXERCISE 4C

Construct sentences of your own using the helping verbs listed below.

1. can: _____

_____

2. must: _____

_____

3. will: _____

_____

4. should: _____

_____

5. has: _____

_____

6. was: _____

_____

Construct a sentence for each of the following patterns. Make certain that the order of the subjects and verbs in your sentences is the same as the order in the pattern. Use as many different helping and main verbs as possible.

S = subject   HV = helping verb   MV = main verb

7. S - MV:

8. S - MV - MV:

9. S - HV - MV:

10. S - HV - HV - MV:

11. S - HV - HV - HV - MV:

12. HV - S - MV? (Notice that this pattern produces a question, not a statement.)

Subject–Verb Identification
Unit Review

Underline the subjects of the following sentences *once* and the verbs *twice*. Some sentences have more than one subject, more than one verb, or both.

Down through the ages, people have loved to wear jewelry. Ancient burial sites reveal an interesting fact. Humans were wearing jewelry before they invented clothing. Until very recently, jewelry was used more for social, political, and religious purposes than for pure decoration. Take finger rings, for example. To what uses have rings been put in the history of mankind?

In the Indus Valley of India, bronze, silver, and gold rings were being made 4500 years ago. In Egypt after 1600 B.C., certain rings were reserved to certain classes of people as symbols of status. The Egyptians also exchanged their rings as pledges and sometimes used them as money. The Egyptians were probably the first to use signet rings. The imprint of a signet ring on a document would serve as the signature of someone in authority.

As Greece became civilized, gold bands became very popular as rings. Also in wide use in early Greece were talismanic rings. These rings were engraved with mystical symbols and were supposed to protect the wearer from harm and to bring good luck.

The Romans regulated rings by law. At first the common people could wear only iron rings, while gold rings were reserved to those of high rank. Later any freeborn citizen could wear a gold ring, freedmen (former slaves) could wear silver, and slaves could wear only iron. The Romans were probably the first to use rings to carry poison. This handy piece of jewelry worked equally well for assassination or for suicide in case of capture during war.

The Egyptians, Greeks, and Romans all used betrothal rings to seal engagements. This custom was adopted by second-century Christians. Later the Christians added a second ring for the wedding ceremony.

During the Middle Ages in Europe, kings at their coronations and bishops at their consecrations were given special rings to symbolize their new power and authority. Today each new pope still receives a gold seal ring. On the ring is carved an image of St. Peter in a fishing boat. When each pope dies, his ring is destroyed.

Rings are as popular as ever, but many rings today are strictly decorative. Do you wear rings? What do they mean to you?

UNIT TWO

Subject–Verb Agreement

5 Recognizing Singular and Plural Subjects and Verbs

Errors in subject–verb agreement are among the most common grammatical mistakes. By applying the rules in this unit, you should be able to correct many of the errors in your own writing.

As you already know, a sentence must contain both a subject and a verb. Read the following two sentences. What is the grammatical difference between them?

The restaurant opens at noon.
The restaurants open at noon.

In the first sentence, the subject *restaurant* is **singular. Singular** means "one." There is only *one* restaurant in the first sentence. In the second sentence, the subject *restaurants* is **plural. Plural** means "two or more." There are at least two (and possibly more than two) restaurants in the second sentence.

Like the subject *restaurant,* the verb *opens* in the first sentence is **singular.** Verb forms ending in *s* are used with *singular* subjects, as in the sentence "The restaurant *accepts* credit cards." The verb *open* in the second sentence is

plural. This verb form (without a final *s*) is used with *plural* subjects, as in the sentence "The restaurants *accept* credit cards."

In other words, if the subject of a sentence is *singular,* the verb in the sentence must also be *singular*. If the subject of the sentence is *plural,* the verb must be *plural*. This matching of singular subjects with singular verbs and plural subjects with plural verbs is called **subject–verb agreement.**

In order to avoid making mistakes in subject–verb agreement, you must be able to recognize the difference between singular and plural subjects and verbs.

The subjects of sentences are usually nouns or pronouns. As you know, the plurals of nouns are usually formed by adding an *s* to singular forms.

Singular	*Plural*
envelope	envelopes
restaurant	restaurants

However, some nouns have irregular plural forms, such as:

Singular	*Plural*
man	men
child	children
leaf	leaves
medium	media (as in the "mass media")
thesis	theses

Those pronouns that can be used as subjects are also singular or plural, depending upon whether they refer to one or to more than one person or thing.

Singular	*Plural*
I	we
you	you
he, she, it	they

Notice that the pronoun *you* may be either singular or plural.

Although adding an *s* to most nouns makes those nouns plural, adding an *s* to a verb makes the verb *singular.*

Four nurses *care* for all the patients.
(plural subject and plural verb)

One nurse *cares* for all the patients.

(singular subject and singular verb)

An easy way to remember this construction is to memorize the following rule:

Any verb ending in s **is** singular.

There are no exceptions to this rule. Therefore, it would be incorrect to have a sentence in which a plural subject is matched with a verb ending in *s*.

INCORRECT   The books *costs* ten dollars.

CORRECT   The books *cost* ten dollars.

INCORRECT   They *needs* money.

CORRECT   They *need* money.

(Remember that the principle behind subject–verb agreement is *not* to match subjects that end in *s* with verbs that end in *s* but to match singular subjects, which usually do *not* end in *s,* with singular verbs, which *do* end in *s.* Similarly, plural subjects, which usually *do* end in *s,* are matched with plural verbs, which do *not* end in *s.*)

In order to avoid subject–verb agreement errors, there are a few rules that you should keep in mind. (How you "keep rules in mind" is up to you. If you find that even after you study rules, you still cannot remember them, you should *memorize* the rules in this unit.)

1. A verb agrees with the subject, not with the complement. A **complement** is a word that refers to the same person or thing as the subject of the sentence. It follows a linking verb.

    Our main *problem is* high prices.

In the sentence above, the subject is *problem*, which is singular. The subject is not *prices*. Rather, *prices* is the complement. Therefore, the verb takes the singular form *is*. If the sentence is reversed, it reads:

    High *prices are* our main problem.

The subject is now the plural noun *prices,* and *problem* is the complement. The verb now takes the plural form *are*. Which are the correct verbs in the following sentences?

The topic of conversation (was, were) the latest movies.
Beans (is, are) the main ingredient in this recipe.

2. Prepositional phrases have no effect on a verb.

    A *woman* with four children *lives* in that house.

In the sentence above, the subject is singular *(woman)*. The prepositional phrase *with four children* has no effect on the verb, which remains singular *(lives)*.

    One of the colleges *has* a soccer team.

The singular verb *has* agrees with the singular subject *one,* not with the plural object of the preposition *(colleges)*. Which are the correct verbs in the following sentences?

    The length of women's skirts (seems, seem) to change every year.
    A hamburger with French fries (costs, cost) a dollar.

3. The following **indefinite pronouns** are singular and require singular verbs. (These pronouns are called *indefinite* because they do not refer to a specific person or to a definite thing, as do subject pronouns such as *he, she,* or *it.*)

    anybody, anyone, anything
    each, each one
    either, neither
    everybody, everyone, everything
    nobody, no one, nothing
    somebody, someone, something

    Everybody likes you.
    Each of these jobs *pays* the minimum wage.
    Either of those times *is* all right with me.

Notice that in the last two sentences, the verbs agree with the singular subjects *each* and *either*. The verbs are not affected by the plural nouns in the prepositional phrases *of these jobs* or *of those times*.

4. When *each, every,* or *any* is used as an adjective, the subjects it modifies require a *singular* verb.

Every automobile and motorcycle *needs* license plates.
Each cafe and restaurant *is inspected* by the Board of Health.

Notice that the adjectives *every* and *each* make the verbs in the sentences singular even though each sentence has more than one subject.

EXERCISE 5A

Circle the verb that correctly completes each sentence. Make certain that you have identified the correct subject of the sentence and that you have crossed out prepositional phrases.

1. London's subway (was, were) completed in 1863.

2. This (make, makes) it the oldest subway in the world.

3. Many other cities with congested traffic (has, have) copied London's underground railway.

4. The first subway in the United States (was, were) built in Boston in 1898.

5. Paris (was, were) not far behind in 1900.

6. The subways of some cities (forms, form) a network rather than a single line.

7. The network of Paris' subways (look, looks) like a giant spiderweb.

8. The subway network of New York (include, includes) over two hundred miles of track.

9. Moscow residents (seems, seem) very proud of their subways.

10. Beautiful slabs of marble (was, were) used to construct the stations.

11. Almost every famous painter and sculptor of Russia (was, were) asked to help in the decorations.

12. Most subway trains (consist, consists) of a number of cars.

13. Each of these cars (has, have) its own engine.

14. An operator at either end of the train (control, controls) all the cars.

15. A new subway system for commuters in the San Francisco area (is, are) controlled automatically by computers.

16. After a shaky start, the San Francisco subways now (carry, carries) many thousands each day.

17. Many cities of the world (plan, plans) to build new subways to meet the demand for better rapid-transit systems.

EXERCISE 5B

Some of the sentences in this exercise contain subject–verb agreement errors. Others are correct as written. If the sentence contains a subject–verb agreement error, cross out the incorrect verb, and write the correct verb in its place. If the sentence is correct, write a *C* in the margin by the sentence number.

1. Each of Mary's dresses are washable.

2. Do either of you want this piece of cake?

3. At this resort, a guest with the right connections get the choice room.

4. The result of his actions was a divorce.

5. In most states, every man and woman over eighteen is free to marry without parental consent.

6. Her main concern right now are plans for the party.

7. Her secret in the beauty contests was never revealed to the other contestants.

8. Any soldier, sailor, airman, and marine with an honorable discharge have various benefits.

9. Everybody in the front three rows gets to come on stage.

10. His tactics in this final match consists of delay and deception.

11. The most important subject in the exams was derivation of square roots.

12. The engine of these newer models with smog devices use too much fuel.

13. Each one of the victims were giving a different story about the incident.

14. Anything in the store windows are available at a discount.

EXERCISE 5C

In the following sentences change each plural subject to its singular form and change each singular subject to its plural form. As you change each subject, change its verb to agree with it. The first sentence has been done as an example.

       brother works
1. My ~~brothers work~~ in the city.

2. The baker bakes delicious pastries.

3. Her plant is my favorite.

4. The sound in the tunnel was too loud.

5. The man in pajamas walks out to get the newspaper.

6. The leader of the group is arguing.

7. His main reason for his answer was unacceptable.

8. The happy song with those Latin rhythms makes her music successful.

9. The main dishes are homemade.

10. The unfortunate result of the crash of the jets was photographed for the news.

11. His tooth shines in the light.

12. Her bracelet costs a fortune.

6 How Conjunctions and Words Such as <u>There</u> Affect Agreement

Here are additional rules that will help you to determine whether a subject is singular or plural.

5. Two subjects joined by the conjunction *and* are **plural** and require a **plural** verb.

   Maine and *Idaho* both *grow* large amounts of potatoes.

6. Two singular subjects joined by the conjunctions *or* or *nor* are **singular** and require a **singular** verb.

   Soup or *salad is included* with your meal.
   Neither the *supermarket* nor the *drugstore sells* nails.

7. If both a singular and a plural subject are joined by *or* or *nor,* the subject that is closer to the verb determines whether the verb is singular or plural.

   Either travelers *checks* or a credit *card is accepted* at this hotel.
   Either a credit *card* or travelers *checks are accepted* at this hotel.

Are travelers checks or a credit *card accepted* at this hotel?
Is a credit card or travelers checks *accepted* at this hotel?

8. In questions and in statements with *there* or *here,* the subject of the sentence *follows* the verb. The words *there* and *here,* as well as interrogatives such as *where, when,* and *how,* are never the subject of the sentence.

    There *are* many amusement *parks* in southern California.
    Here *are* your *keys.*
    Where *was* your *wallet?*
    When *does* your *plane leave?*
    How *have* your *children been?*

EXERCISE 6A

Circle the verb that correctly completes each sentence.

1. There (is, are) some displays you must see.

2. Neither Jane nor Mary (like, likes) the end of the movie.

3. Each man and woman in the room (have, has) something to say.

4. The rhythm of the song and its lyrics (was, were) very appealing.

5. Here (is, are) the first five answers to your questions.

6. Which (is, are) the causes of her anxiety?

7. Their reactions to the joke (were, was) understandable.

8. Johnson and Jackson (has, have) made up their minds.

9. Either a quarter or a transfer with today's date (pays, pay) for this ride.

10. Mistakes in the placement of new employees (occur, occurs) frequently.

11. Neither wild horses nor a rain storm (keep, keeps) her from jogging every day.

12. Somebody with high heels (is, are) dancing upstairs.

13. (Is, Are) your nephews or your uncle going to meet you?

14. Everyone in her classes (enjoy, enjoys) her lectures.

15. Movies and television (takes, take) up all his spare time.

EXERCISE 6B

Some of the sentences in this exercise contain subject–verb agreement errors. Others are correct as written. If a sentence contains a subject–verb agreement error, cross out the incorrect verb, and write the correct verb in its place. If a sentence is correct, write *C* in the margin by the sentence number.

1. Our century is an age of technological marvels.

2. Sometimes the complexity of our inventions take the simple joy out of using them.

3. Then inventors and inventions has to go back to the principle of simplicity.

4. Several recent examples of this pleasure-from-simplicity principle comes to mind.

5. Most modern sailing yachts are marvels of naval architecture and engineering.

6. But too many modern sailboats spend days or weeks out of action because complex parts or electronic equipment break down.

7. Today a new generation of much simpler sailboats have created millions of new sailors.

8. Sailing enthusiasts claim that of all the new boats the simplest and most pleasurable ones is the sailboards.

9. The rider of a sailboard become one with his boat because his body controls the speed and direction of the craft.

10. Similar trends in simplicity has taken place in the sport of flying.

11. Glider pilots have always believed that gliding was more fun than fly-ing airplanes.

12. New developments in design and the use of new and stronger materials has produced the hang glider.

13. The man on a hang glider is flying a very efficient and, usually, con-trollable kite.

14. Neither sailboards nor the hang glider need any power but air currents.

15. Each one of these devices require constant and delicate adjustment to changing conditions, but this responsiveness is the source of the user's pleasure.

16. Here is a final example of joy in simplicity.

17. A group of touring American athletes recently spent six weeks in the People's Republic of China.

18. Neither their high-tech sports equipment nor their headset stereos were the great attraction.

19. Wherever the athletes went in China, the favorite American invention were Frisbees!

EXERCISE 6C

In the following sentences change all singular subjects to their plural form and all plural subjects to their singular form. If this change affects subject–verb agreement, then change the verb to match the new subject. The first sentence has been done as an example.

                          are   openings
1. There ~~is~~ no ~~opening~~ at the Kordox Corporation.

2. The rolls and the pie are done.

3. Neither the lemon nor the orange was ripe.

4. Here is the answer to your question.

5. The best restaurant is closed for the winter.

6. Either the decoration or the lights need to be changed.

7. Victory is her goal.

8. Neither the trucks nor the car was parked in the right place.

9. The boys and the cat are playmates.

10. The cat is friendly with the boys.

11. Neither the saws nor the hammers belong to John.

12. The lifeguard, with help from others, is looking for the child.

13. Where is your soup bowl?

7 Additional Singular and Plural Words and Inverted Sentences

The following are some final rules concerning subject–verb agreement.

9. Some words, though plural in form, are singular in meaning and therefore require a **singular** verb. Such words include *news, mathematics, physics, economics, mumps,* and *measles.*

   Mathematics is a required subject for engineering majors.
   Mumps makes it difficult to swallow.

10. A unit of time, weight, measurement, or money usually requires a **singular** verb because the entire amount is thought of as a single unit.

    Two *hours was* not long enough for that test.
    Fifty *dollars seems* a reasonable price for that jacket.
    Four *ounces* of chocolate *is needed* for this recipe.

11. Collective nouns usually require **singular** verbs. A **collective noun** is a word that is singular in form but that refers to a group of people or things. Some common collective nouns are words such as *group, team, family, class, crowd,* and *committee.*

The *team practices* every afternoon.
The *crowd has been* very noisy.

Occasionally, a collective noun may be used with a plural verb if the writer wishes to show that the members of the group are acting as separate individuals rather than as a unified body. Notice the difference in meaning between the following pair of sentences.

The *City Council has agreed* to raise taxes. (In this sentence, the City Council is acting as a single, unified group.)
The *City Council are arguing* over a proposal to raise taxes. (In this sentence, the City Council is viewed as a collection of separate individuals who, because they are not in agreement, are not acting as a unified group.)

12. Indefinite pronouns, such as the words *some, half, all,* and *most* may take either singular or plural verbs, depending upon their meaning. If these words tell *how much* of something is meant, the verb is singular. If they tell *how many* of something is meant, the verb is plural.

Most of the milk *is* sour. (how much)
Most of the oranges *are* sour. (how many)
Some of the land *contains* gold. (how much)
Some of the boxes *contain* money. (how many)
All of the hospital *has* air conditioning. (how much)
All of my children *have* the flu. (how many)

(Do not confuse the words in this rule with the words *each, either,* and *neither* in Rule 3. These three words *always* require a *singular* verb.)

13. Some sentences have an inverted pattern in which the verb precedes the subject. Be especially careful to check for subject–verb agreement in this type of sentence.

Among his most valuable possessions *is* an antique *car.* (If the order of this sentence were reversed, it would read, "An antique *car is* among his most valuable possessions.")
In the middle of the wall *hang* two large *paintings.* (Two large *paintings hang* in the middle of the wall.)

Main or helping verbs may also precede subjects in questions.

Are you happy?
Does anyone know the date?
Have they bought a house yet?

5, 6, 7.

EXERCISE 7A

Circle the verb that correctly completes each sentence.

1. Fifty cents for a doughnut (is, are) too much!

2. A group of tourists (leaves, leave) every hour.

3. (Do, Does) any of the children resemble the parents?
   He, She.

4. Their team (practices, practice) two hours a day.

5. Most of the items in the catalog (sell, sells) for under a hundred
   dollars.

6. One hundred pounds per person (are, is) the maximum allowance for
   luggage.

7. Physics (are, is) her favorite subject.

8. The committee (consists, consist) of one person from each class.

9. Within each package (is, are) two or more coupons.

10. The Board of Trustees (argue, argues) during their meetings.

11. Some of the rice (were, was) spilled.

12. Among the winners of the contest (were, was) a winner from last year.

13. Measles usually (cause, causes) a fever.

14. Four cups of heavy cream (makes, make) the recipe very rich.

15. Part of the faculty (help, helps) with the talent show.

EXERCISE 7B

Some of the sentences in this exercise contain subject–verb agreement errors. Others are correct as written. If the sentence contains a subject–verb agreement error, cross out the incorrect verb, and write the correct form in its place. If the sentence is correct, write *C* in the margin by the sentence number. This exercise covers rules from Lessons 5–7.

1. For many people the comics is the most important part of the newspaper.

2. Although the humor of some comic strips is often shallow, many of these strips makes serious criticisms of our society.

3. One of the first of these strips were created by R. F. Outcault in the 1890s, and much of the humor of "Hogan's Alley" dealt with the problems of America's new immigrants.

4. Many of today's comic strips are drawn by some of our society's most observant critics.

5. "Cathy" by Cathy Guisewite and the more recent "Sally Forth" explores with biting humor the special concerns of women.

6. Since 1970 there have been a large number of newspapers with "Quincy" by Harlem-born cartoonist Ted Shearer, and, not surprisingly, this strip sees life from the viewpoint of the ghetto.

7. Because today's top cartoonists are syndicated in hundreds of cities, they can dare to be free of a single newspaper or of a single region.

8. At the very top of the daring strips are certainly ''Doonesbury'' by Garry Trudeau.

9. ''Doonesbury'' was first syndicated in 1970 and have jumped feet first into every national debate ever since.

10. The Vietnam War, the Watergate scandal, women's liberation, and President Reagan's budget problems has provided some of the targets for Trudeau's pen.

11. Neither Democrats nor Republicans escapes from ''Doonesbury,'' and a great collection of foreign leaders have been ridiculed like their American counterparts.

12. Some newspaper editors occasionally deletes ''Doonesbury'' for a single issue or drops it temporarily.

13. But the large readership of ''Doonesbury'' and the success of many other so-called serious strips seems to indicate an American preference for ''comics'' about the people's deepest concerns.

EXERCISE 7C

Some of the sentences in this exercise contain subject–verb agreement errors. Others are correct as written. If the sentence contains a subject–verb agreement error, cross out the incorrect verb, and write the correct form in its place. If the sentence is correct, write *C* in the margin by the sentence number. This exercise covers rules from Lessons 5–7.

1. There come the winners.

2. Some of her research are questionable.

3. The executive board meet every Friday.

4. His physics assignments take three hours to do.

5. Four dollars are the cost of the concert.

6. Many of Lisa's questions were answered.

7. Most of the fruit have been delicious.

8. Do either of your brothers like pizza?

9. Twelve pounds of hamburger appear to be enough for the picnic.

10. Good news makes a happy messenger.

11. Part of the cheese is missing.

12. Have her group been photographed?

Subject–Verb Agreement
Unit Review

Correct any subject–verb agreement errors that you find in the following essay by crossing out the incorrect verb and writing in the correct form. It may help you to underline all the subjects in the essay *once* and all the verbs *twice* before you try to identify errors in agreement.

Circus mean "ring" in Latin. The original Roman circuses of 2,000 years ago were large round structures for horse and chariot races. Many of the rows of seats in the Circus Maximus is standing today. The Roman games and races in the Circus were often bloody and violent.

Many circuses nowadays takes place in a large tent. Circuses of this type began as traveling shows in the eighteenth century. The central attraction at first were trained horses. Other trained animals, acrobats, and clowns were added later. Everybody, no matter how rich or poor, were able to afford these entertainments.

Today's circus, with its hundreds of employees, often have numerous tents. The main tent is known as the big top. Around this main tent is perhaps a freak show, various concessions, and cages of wild animals.

Russia has a network of state-supported traveling circuses. Almost every boy and girl in Russia hope to see one of these shows. And the circus performers of each traveling show hope to qualify someday for the big Moscow Circus in the capital city. Of course, the performers in the Moscow Circus earns the very highest salaries.

Today circuses everywhere must compete with many other forms of entertainment. Although the popularity of circuses have gone down in recent years, there are always a group of people in love with the smell of sawdust and popcorn and the sight of tigers and acrobats.

The largest and best known circus in the United States now are called "Ringling Brothers and Barnum and Bailey's Circus." At one time the famous names in this title represented three competing circuses, but now this trio are a single company. It plays only very large cities like New York. When it plays in Madison Square Garden or other permanent structures, there are no need for the big tents, and many in the audience is seated far from the horses, lions, and clowns.

Compound and Complex Sentences Versus Run-On Sentences and Fragments

8 Compound Sentences

A **compound sentence,** as you learned in Lesson 2 (p. 16), contains *at least two subjects and two verbs,* usually arranged in an S-V/S-V pattern. For example:

CONNECT by CONJ

    S   V   S V
The museum needed more money, so it raised its admission fees.

 S   V   S   V
We wanted to go on a picnic, but a rainstorm changed our plans.

In grammar, the term **compound** means "having two or more parts." Thus, the sentence "My *brother* and his *wife* are both engineers" has a **compound subject.** "The car *ran* out of gas and *stalled* in the intersection" has a **compound verb.**

A compound sentence can be divided into two parts, each of which can be a separate sentence by itself.

The museum needed more money.

       +

It raised its admission fees.

We wanted to go on a picnic.

+

A rainstorm changed our plans.

Since a compound sentence can be divided into *two* separate sentences, each half of a compound sentence must contain at least one subject and one verb. Therefore, each half of a compound sentence is a **clause.** A clause is a group of words that contains both a subject and a verb. (In contrast, a group of words that does not contain both a subject and a verb is called a **phrase,** as in a prepositional phrase.) A clause that can stand alone as a complete sentence is called an **independent clause.** Since each clause in a compound sentence can stand alone as a complete sentence, each clause must be independent. In other words:

A compound sentence consists of at least two independent clauses joined together to form a single sentence.

There are two ways to join independent clauses in order to form a compound sentence. The most frequently used method is to put a conjunction between the clauses. A **conjunction** is a word that joins words or groups of words. In grammar, the word *coordinate* means "of equal importance." Therefore, the conjunctions that are used in compound sentences are called **coordinating conjunctions** because they join two groups of words that are of equal grammatical importance. (They are both independent clauses.) The following coordinating conjunctions are used to join the clauses of compound sentences:

and
but
for (when used as a synonym for *because* rather than as a preposition)
nor
or
so
yet

You should *memorize* these coordinating conjunctions because later you will have to be able to distinguish between them and the conjunctions that are used to form complex sentences (p. 17).

In the following sentences, underline the subjects of the compound sentences *once* and the verbs *twice,* and circle the coordinating conjunction that joins the clauses. Notice that a comma precedes the coordinating conjunction.

The curtain rose, and the play began.

The professor asked a question, but no one knew the answer.

I no longer eat desserts, for I am trying to lose weight.

The neighbors haven't seen your dog, nor have I. (Notice that when *nor* is

used to join two independent clauses, the pattern becomes S-V/V-S:

He has no children, nor *has she.*)

You should put more money in the parking meter, or you may get a ticket.

The lifeguard spotted a shark near the shore, so the beach was closed.

He earns a good salary, yet he always wants to borrow money from his

friends.

Construct compound sentences of your own, using the coordinating conjunctions listed below to join your clauses. Underline the subject of each clause *once* and the verb *twice.* (You may construct a clause that has more than one subject and/or more than one verb, but each clause must have *at least* one subject and one verb.)

_____, and _____

_____, but _____

_____, for _____

_____, or _____

The second way to join the clauses in a compound sentence is to use a semicolon (;) *in place of both the comma and the coordinating conjunction.* For example:

My car won't start; the battery must be dead.
You should water the garden; the plants are wilting in the heat.

Compound sentences constructed with semicolons occur less frequently than compound sentences constructed with coordinating conjunctions because a conjunction is usually needed to show the relationship between the clauses. For example, without a coordinating conjunction the logical relationship between the two clauses in the following sentence might be confusing.

The cashier charged me $25; the bill was incorrect.

If, however, you replace the semicolon with a coordinating conjunction, the relationship between the clauses becomes clear.

The cashier charged me $25, *but* the bill was incorrect.

Therefore, when you construct compound sentences of your own, use semicolons only when the relationship between the clauses is clear even without the use of a coordinating conjunction.

Construct two compound sentences of your own, using semicolons to join the clauses. Underline the subjects *once* and the verbs *twice*. Make certain that each clause has at least one subject and one verb.

_____ ; _____

_____ ; _____

As you can see from the sentences that you have constructed, the following punctuation rules apply to compound sentences:

1. If the clauses in a compound sentence are joined by a coordinating conjunction, place a comma before (to the left of) the conjunction.

This sentence is compound, and it contains a comma.

You may have learned that it is not necessary to use commas in short compound sentences (for example, ''He's a Scorpio and I'm a Libra''). Although this is true, not everyone agrees on how short a ''short'' compound sentence is, so if you are in doubt, it is safer to use a comma. All the sentences in the exercises for this unit will be ''long'' compound sentences and should have a comma before the conjunction.

2. Although a compound sentence may contain more than one conjunction, the comma is placed only before the conjunction that joins the clauses.

Judy *and* Joan are identical twins, *and* I can't tell them apart.

3. If the clauses in a compound sentence are *not* joined by a coordinating conjunction, place a semicolon between the clauses.

I know your name; I just can't remember it at the moment.

The following sentence patterns do *not* require commas because they are **simple** (meaning that they contain only one clause) rather than compound.

S-V-V	The nurse took my temperature and checked my blood pressure. (no comma)
S-S-V	Agriculture and tourism are two of Hawaii's main industries. (no comma)
S-S-V-V	My sister and I went to Europe and stayed there for three months. (no comma)

To review, the two patterns for punctuating a compound sentence are:

clause + comma + coordinating conjunction + clause
The boxer was badly injured, so the referee stopped the fight.

clause + semicolon + clause
I'm not sleeping; I'm just resting my eyelids.

EXERCISE 8A

Make each of the following independent clauses a compound sentence by adding an appropriate coordinating conjunction and a second independent clause. Try to use as many different conjunctions in this exercise as possible. Remember to place a comma before the coordinating conjunction.

1. The fog rolled in early _____

_____

2. Mary wants to be a nurse _____

_____

3. Lunch is served at noon _____

_____

4. The doctor rode in the ambulance _____

_____

5. Bill's team scored 87 points _____

_____

Write compound sentences of your own, using the coordinating conjunctions listed below. Remember to place a comma before the coordinating conjunction that divides the clauses, and make certain that each of your clauses contains at least one subject and one verb.

6. but: _____

_____

7. so: _____

_____

8. and: _____

_____

9. or: _____

_____

10. nor: _____

_____

11. for: _____

_____

12. yet: _____

_____

Construct two compound sentences of your own, punctuated with semicolons.

13. _____

_____

14. _____

_____

✓ EXERCISE 8B

Add commas and semicolons to the following sentences wherever they are needed. If a sentence needs no additional punctuation (in other words, if the sentence is simple rather than compound), label it *C* for *correct*.

1. No one knows who invented the needle; it was probably made from a bone or a sliver of stone.

2. From that simple invention, needlework has developed into a great variety of forms. *C*

3. The most creative forms are used for decorative purposes; these forms are of three general types.

4. The design may use the original threads of the material, or it may use new threads worked into a base fabric, or it may involve the stitching of a separate piece of cloth, or other objects to a base fabric.

5. *Knitting* and *crocheting* are two examples of the first type; both employ large needles and heavy thread or yarn.

6. In knitting, the needles are moved with the hands to create a series of interlocking loops; in crocheting some of the loops are pulled through other, preceding loops with a hooked needle.

7. The second general type of needlework is called *embroidery*, and references to it may be found in the oldest scriptures of India, and the book of Exodus in the Old Testament.

8. Embroidery varies according to the type of materials and to the type of stitching. *C*

9. The most prized embroidery in Asia uses silk threads on a silk base fabric with stitches almost invisible to the human eye. *C*

10. *Needlepoint* embroidery sews large diagonal stitches of various threads into canvas one of the most popular recent books on needlepoint was written by all-American and all-Pro lineman Rosey Grier.

11. The third general type of decorative needlework is illustrated by *patchwork quilts* the design of these quilts is created by sewing various colored patches into patterns.

12. These patterns are often very intricate and some create an illusion of three dimensions on the flat surface of the quilt.

13. At various times in history, almost every conceivable object has been sewn to cloth to create designs in medieval Europe pearls, rubies and other precious stones were combined with embroidery to create the richly decorated clothes of the powerful and wealthy.

14. Most cloth today is created on amazing computer-controlled machines but needlework in all its amazing variety continues to occupy the hands and eyes of many people around the world.

EXERCISE 8C

All the sentence patterns listed below have multiple subjects, multiple verbs, or both. But some patterns are for *simple* sentences, and other patterns are for *compound* sentences. Write a sentence for each pattern. If a sentence is *compound,* apply one of the two punctuation rules for compound sentences.

1. S-V-V: _____

_____

2. S-V-S-V: _____

_____

3. S-V-V-S-V: _____

_____

4. S-S-V: _____

_____

5. S-V-V-V: _____

_____

6. S-V-S-S-V: _____

_____

7. S-S-V-V: _____

_____

8. S-S-V-S-V: _____

_____

9 Complex Sentences

There are two kinds of clauses, independent and dependent. As you have seen in Lesson 8, **independent clauses** can stand alone as complete sentences. For example:

Many tourists visit the Grand Canyon.
Insects have six legs.

A **dependent clause,** however, *cannot* stand alone as a complete sentence. Instead, it must be attached to, or *depend* upon, an *independent* clause in order to form a grammatically complete sentence and to express a complete idea. Notice that the following dependent clauses are *not* complete sentences.

As the movie ended . . .
When you graduate from college . . .
If you inherit a million dollars . . .

These clauses seem incomplete because they are actually only *half* of a sentence. Using the first of the following sentences as a model, change each dependent clause into a complete sentence by adding an appropriate *independent* clause.

As the movie ended, _____ *the audience cheered.*_____

When you graduate from college, _____

_____ .

If you inherit a million dollars, _____

_____ .

You have now constructed two complex sentences. A **complex sentence** contains both independent and dependent clauses. (In contrast, a **compound sentence** contains only *independent* clauses.)

Every dependent clause begins with a subordinating conjunction. A **conjunction** joins words or groups of words. The conjunctions that begin dependent clauses are called **subordinating conjunctions** because the word *subordinate* means "of lesser importance." Grammatically speaking, a dependent clause is "less important" than an independent clause because it cannot stand alone as a complete sentence. In contrast, the conjunctions that you used in the previous lesson to form compound sentences are called **coordinating conjunctions** because *coordinate* means "of equal importance." Since both of the clauses in a compound sentence are independent, both clauses are "of equal importance."

The type of dependent clause that you will be studying in this lesson is called an **adverb clause** because, like an adverb, an adverb clause describes a verb (or sometimes an adjective or an adverb). It is the same kind of clause that you worked with in Lesson 2, pages 17–18. The subordinating conjunctions used to begin adverb clauses describe verbs by telling *how, when, where, why* or *under what conditions* the action occurs.

how: as if, as though
when: after, as, as soon as, before, until, when, whenever, while
where: where, wherever
why: because, in order that, since, so that
under what conditions: although, as long as, even though, if, though, unless

Read the following sentences. A slanted line indicates the point at which each sentence divides into two separate clauses. Underline the subject of each clause *once* and the verb *twice*. Circle the subordinating conjunction.

Whenever we have a picnic,/ we always eat potato salad.

Because he is my friend,/ I trust him completely.

Some people left the stadium/ before the game ended.

Now examine the clause in each sentence that contains the circled subordinating conjunction.

The clause that contains the subordinating conjunction is the dependent clause.

Notice that in a complex sentence, the dependent clause may be either the first or the second clause in the sentence.

If you like mysteries, you should read the novels of Agatha Christie.
I waited at the airport for two hours *until the plane arrived.*

In most cases, the adverb clauses in a complex sentence are *reversible.* That is, the sentence has the same basic meaning no matter which clause comes first. For example:

After we finish dinner, we'll go to the park.
>   or
We'll go to the park *after we finish dinner.*

I went to the dentist *because my tooth ached.*
>   or
Because my tooth ached, I went to the dentist.

However, the order of the clauses in a complex sentence does affect the punctuation of the sentence.

1. If the **dependent** clause is the first clause in the sentence, it is followed by a comma.

    Before she went to Europe, she applied for a passport.

2. If the **independent** clause is the first clause in the sentence, no comma is needed.

She applied for a passport *before she went to Europe*. (no comma)

Punctuate the following complex sentences. First circle the subordinating conjunction in each sentence, and draw a slanted line between the clauses.

conj → As soon as the guest of honor arrives / we can begin the party.

He spoke loudly / so that everyone could hear him.

Although my car is old / it still runs well.

While you are on vacation / I'll water your lawn.

The highways will be crowded / since today is a holiday.

EXERCISE 9A

Complete each of the following complex sentences by adding an appropriate adverb clause (one that makes sense in the sentence). Add commas where they are necessary.

1. After _____

   Bobby left the stadium.

2. The president will be reelected if _____

   _____.

3. Sharon loved coffee although _____

   _____.

4. When _____

   the reporters rushed outside.

5. As soon as _____

   _____ it rained.

Construct complex sentences of your own, using the following subordinating conjunctions to form your adverb clauses. Add commas where they are necessary.

6. _____ wherever

   _____.

7. _____ so that

   _____.

8. _____ even though

_____ .

9. _____ since

_____ .

10. Because _____

_____ .

EXERCISE 9B

First underline the dependent clauses in the following complex sentences. Then add commas to the sentences if they are necessary. If a sentence needs no additional punctuation, label it *C* for *correct*.

1. As the years go by, more and more Americans are seeking to condition their bodies by exercise.

2. Unfortunately, too many of these exercisers quit their conditioning programs because the programs do not fit their individual needs.

3. A good program will clearly improve the body's condition each week although it will never push the body beyond the limits of its endurance.

4. Now a simple test has been developed so that exercisers can determine the precise pace for conditioning their own bodies.

5. Because the test uses only the exerciser's pulse and a watch with a second hand it can be performed anywhere.

6. So that we can understand the simplicity of the test let's use the example of thirty-year-old Mary Jones.

7. After she has compared herself with some of her friends Mary decides to condition her body by walking and jogging.

8. She first calculates her Training Heart Rate. *C*

9. After she subtracts her age of 30 from the base rate of 220 Mary gets a Training Heart Rate of 190.

10. Since she is not in good condition she trains for the first month at 60 percent of 190 for a pulse rate of 115.

11. She takes a fast ten-minute walk for three days each week so that her pulse rises to 115 beats per minute.

12. After Mary does this for a month she is ready for the second month at 70 percent of her Training Heart Rate or a pulse of 135.

13. Because her heart is getting stronger it does more work with less effort.

14. Now Mary may have to jog instead of walk so that her pulse will reach the new rate of 135.

15. After her second month of conditioning, Mary is ready to exercise at a higher pulse rate of 80 percent of her Training Heart Rate.

16. Although she could go on eventually to 100 percent of her Training Heart Rate an 80 percent rate will get Mary in excellent condition.

17. If she's willing she can maintain this new strength and energy for the rest of her life.

18. This method of pacing a conditioning program works for all ages and for any exercise to speed up the heart pump.

19. Because it never stops the heart is our best indicator of good physical condition.

EXERCISE 9C

For each different *type* of subordinating conjunction, write a complex sentence with an adverb clause. The adverb clause may come at the beginning or at the end of the sentence.

1. a subordinating conjunction that shows *why* the action occurs:

_____

_____

2. a subordinating conjunction that shows *where* the action occurs:

_____

_____

3. a subordinating conjunction that shows *how* the action occurs:

_____

_____

4. a subordinating conjunction that shows *when* the action occurs:

_____

_____

5. a subordinating conjunction that shows *under what conditions* the action occurs:

_____

_____

10 Avoiding Run-On Sentences and Comma Splices

As you learned in Lesson 8 (p. 82), a compound sentence consists of at least two independent clauses. The independent clauses in a compound sentence must be separated either by a coordinating conjunction (such as *and, but, or*) preceded by a comma or by a semicolon if no conjunction is used.

Failure to separate two independent clauses results in an error known as a **run-on sentence.** The following are examples of run-on sentences.

I had the flu I stayed home from work yesterday.
The team was leading by 10 points in the third quarter it still lost the game.

Run-on sentences are very serious errors. They are not only confusing to the reader, but they also indicate that the writer cannot tell where one sentence ends and another begins.

There are three ways to correct a run-on sentence.

1. Divide the run-on into two separate sentences, ending each sentence with a period. (If the sentences are questions, end them with question marks.)

I had the flu. I stayed home from work yesterday.
The team was leading by 10 points in the third quarter. It still lost the game.

Although this method produces grammatically correct sentences, an essay written completely in short simple sentences creates the choppy effect of an elementary-school reading text. Therefore, you should also consider using the two other methods of correcting run-ons.

2. Change the run-on to a **compound sentence** by separating the clauses with a semicolon or with a coordinating conjunction preceded by a comma.

I had the flu; I stayed home from work yesterday.

or

I had the flu, *so* I stayed home from work yesterday.

The team was leading by 10 points in the third quarter; it still lost the game.

or

The team was leading by 10 points in the third quarter, *but* it still lost the game.

As you learned on page 84, the relationship between the two clauses in a compound sentence is often clearer if a conjunction is used rather than a semicolon.

3. Change the run-on to a **complex sentence** by placing a subordinating conjunction before one of the clauses.

Because I had the flu, I stayed home from work yesterday.
Although the team was leading by 10 points in the third quarter, it still lost the game.

Another very common error is the comma splice. Unlike a run-on, in which two independent clauses are run together with *no* punctuation, a **comma splice** consists of two independent clauses joined with *not enough* punctuation — that is, with only a comma (and *no* coordinating conjunction). The following are examples of comma splices.

You should be careful sunbathing, overexposure to the sun can damage your skin.
Today is a legal holiday, the banks are closed.

A comma by itself is *not* a strong enough punctuation mark to separate two independent clauses. Only periods and semicolons can be used without conjunctions to separate independent clauses. Comma splices can be corrected by the same three methods used for correcting run-on sentences.

1. Divide the comma splice into two separate sentences.

   You should be careful sunbathing. Overexposure to the sun can damage your skin.
   Today is a legal holiday. The banks are closed.

2. Change the comma splice into a **compound sentence** by separating the clauses with either a coordinating conjunction *and* a comma or with a semicolon.

   You should be careful sunbathing, *for* overexposure to the sun can damage your skin.

   or

   You should be careful sunbathing; overexposure to the sun can damage your skin.
   Today is a legal holiday, *and* the banks are closed.

3. Change the comma splice into a **complex sentence** by placing a subordinating conjunction before one of the clauses.

   You should be careful sunbathing *because* overexposure to the sun can damage your skin.
   Since today is a legal holiday, the banks are closed.

Remember that if the dependent clause (the clause containing the subordinating conjunction) is the first clause in the sentence, it should be followed by a comma.

   Correct the following run-on sentences and comma splices.

   Run-on sentences are serious errors you should avoid writing them.

   Stan's checks often bounce he never bothers to balance his checkbook.

   I didn't like that movie it was too violent.

Football is one of the most popular sports in the United States, *(but)* soccer is more popular in other parts of the world.

Many colleges are raising their fees *, but* students are having financial problems.

He must not know how to cook, *because* he always serves his guests frozen TV dinners.

EXERCISE 10A

Correct all the run-on sentences and comma splices in the following exercise. Some sentences are neither run-ons nor comma splices; label these sentences *C* for *correct*.

1. The most popular of all pool games is known as eight-ball, players of all ages enjoy the special challenges of this form of pocket billiards.

2. The game is called eight-ball because both players try to win by sinking that ball in a chosen pocket.

3. However, each player must ''earn'' his chance to shoot at the eight-ball, he must first sink the low set of balls (numbered from 1 to 7) or the high set (from 9 to 15).

4. At the beginning of the game, all fifteen balls are racked at one end of the table in the usual triangular shape with the eight-ball in the very center of the rack.

5. As soon as a player makes a ball from either set, that set becomes his for the rest of the game.

6. One of the attractions of eight-ball is the ever-present chance to snatch victory from almost certain defeat a player with only the eight-ball to shoot will sometimes lose to his opponent's sudden ''run'' of four or five successful shots.

7. Another special feature of eight-ball is certain rules these rules punish the careless player or reward the daring one.

8. For example, a daring and skillful player may win on the opening shot by smashing the rack hard enough to make the eight-ball, but if the cue ball goes in a pocket too, he loses!

9. At any time during the game, a careless player may lose by unintentionally sinking the eight-ball.

10. The most frustrating loss can occur at the very end of a hard-fought game a player might successfully make an unusually difficult shot on the eight-ball and then watch the still-moving cue ball roll slowly into a waiting pocket for a lost game.

11. With its sudden changes of fortune and come-from-behind victories, the game of eight-ball deserves its popularity among pool players.

EXERCISE 10B

Correct all of the run-on sentences and comma splices in the following letter. Do *not* make changes in sentences that are already correctly punctuated.

Dear Mr. Johnson,

My jaw is wrapped in a big bandage, I can't use the telephone, so I'm using this letter to explain my absence from work.

I came up here to Pottsville last weekend to help my uncle on his farm, he wanted me to help him repair the top of his silo. You know what a silo is it's a round brick tower about 40 feet high for storing cattle feed.

My uncle had the flu I had to work by myself. I put a pulley at the top of the silo and ran 100 feet of rope from the ground up to the pulley and back down to a wheelbarrow on the ground. I put some bricks in the wheelbarrow and pulled on the rope. Just as I had the wheelbarrow lifted up near the pulley, my uncle's dog bit me, this made me jerk the rope and caused a bag of cement to fall from the top of the silo right on to my load of bricks, suddenly the wheelbarrow of bricks was heavier than I was I was jerked up into the air. I held on to that rope so I wouldn't fall, but I nearly let go when the wheelbarrow hit me on its way down. Of course, I kept going up and bumped my head on the pulley. Just then the load of bricks hit the ground and spilled that made my end of the rope heavier, down I went, I really held on to that rope even when the wheelbarrow coming up banged into my leg. When I hit the ground, I must have been stunned because I let go of the rope and down came the wheelbarrow it might have killed me, but it hit my uncle's dog first he was trying to bite me again. Now my uncle calls me "Lucky."

I should be out of this hospital in about two weeks, please say "Hello" to all the gang in the office.

Your employee,

Ralph "Lucky" Lumstead

EXERCISE 10C

The length of a sentence does not indicate whether it is *simple, compound,* or *complex.* A simple sentence may be very long. Compound and complex sentences may be very short. Correct all the run-on sentences and comma splices in the following exercise. If a sentence is neither a run-on nor a comma splice, label it *C* for *correct.*

1. Stop!

2. Stop, listen!

3. George is writing.

4. George left Mary left.

5. After George left, Mary left.

6. The green and shiny plant blossomed.

7. Jane kissed old George, Jack scowled.

8. Frank and Ernest worked hard and became rich.

9. The tall woman in the green and yellow dress smiled.

10. As I ate, the food on my plate became increasingly tasteless.

11. The graceful elephants in the ring stood up on their hind legs and saluted the crowd.

12. Paul wanted his sister in Milwaukee to visit him during the week of graduation, she did.

13. The old Chevy had been driven for over 200,000 miles by a series of uncaring drivers it collapsed and died.

14. Many Americans leave the long and cold winters of the northern states for the warm and sunny South or Southwest but then discover some other disadvantage in their new home like air pollution or low wages.

11 Avoiding Fragments

The basic unit of expression in written English is the sentence. As you already know, *a sentence must contain at least one independent clause*.

If you take a group of words that is *not* a complete sentence and punctuate it as though it were a complete sentence, you have created a **sentence fragment.** In other words, you have written only a piece — a fragment — of a sentence rather than a complete sentence.

As you can see. These three groups of words. Are fragments.

Although fragments occur frequently in speech and occasionally in informal writing, they are generally not acceptable in classroom writing and should be avoided in formal writing situations.

There are two types of fragments: **dependent clauses** and **phrases**.

As you have already learned in Lesson 9 (p. 93), a dependent clause cannot stand alone as a complete sentence. It must be attached to an independent clause in order to form a complex sentence.

Therefore, any dependent clause that is not part of a complex sentence is a fragment.

Eliminate the dependent-clause fragments in the following groups of words by making them part of a complex sentence.

We may not get tickets for the rock concert. Unless we order them weeks in advance.

Jerry plans to buy a new car. As soon as he saves enough money.

When you pay your income tax. You should write your Social Security number on your check.

Are you remembering to punctuate your complex sentences correctly? As you learned in Lesson 9, if the *dependent* clause is the first clause in a sentence, it should be followed by a comma. If the *independent* clause is the first clause in a sentence, no comma is needed.

The second type of fragment is the phrase. Since a **phrase** is defined as a group of words that does *not* contain both a subject and a verb, a phrase obviously cannot be a complete sentence. All phrases are fragments. Study the following types of fragments, and notice the way each phrase has been changed from a fragment into a complete sentence.

FRAGMENT—NO SUBJECT	Will return soon.
SENTENCE	*I* will return soon.
FRAGMENT—NO VERB	The football on the 50-yard line.
SENTENCE	The football *is* on the 50-yard line.
FRAGMENT—INCOMPLETE VERB (*-ing* form)	The dog barking all night.
	(An *-ing* verb must be preceded by a helping verb. Or you may change the *-ing* form to a single main verb that can be used without a helping verb.)
SENTENCES	The dog *was barking* all night.
	or
	The dog *barked* all night.
FRAGMENTS—INCOMPLETE VERB (past participle)	John eaten the pizza.
	The poisonous mushrooms picked by the campers.
	(A past participle needs a helping verb in order to form a complete verb. For an explanation and list of past participles, see Lesson 23.)
SENTENCES	John *has eaten* the pizza.
	The poisonous mushrooms *were picked* by the campers.

The following groups of words are fragments because they lack either a subject or a verb or because they have an incomplete verb. Rewrite each fragment so that it becomes a complete sentence.

The hamburgers at McDonald's.

The farmers hoping for more rain.

The child abandoned by her parents.

Received your letter yesterday.

The man standing at the corner.

The ball thrown by the pitcher.

When you are writing a composition, be careful not to separate a phrase from the rest of the sentence to which it belongs.

INCORRECT   She looked through her purse. Trying to find her keys.
CORRECT   She looked through her purse, trying to find her keys.
INCORRECT   Exhausted after the race. The runner collapsed on the track.
CORRECT   Exhausted after the race, the runner collapsed on the track.

Rewrite the following items so that they no longer contain fragments caused by phrases that are incorrectly separated from the sentences to which they belong.

The dog ran into the house. Leaving a trail of muddy paw prints behind it.

Wanting to do well on the exam. Anita studied for three days.

Puzzled by the teacher's question. The entire class sat in silence.

The supermarket started another contest. Hoping to attract new customers.

To summarize: **phrases** are sentence fragments because they do not contain both a subject and a verb (in other words, they are not clauses). **Dependent clauses** are fragments because they are not *independent* clauses. This is simply another way of stating the most basic rule of sentence construction.

Every sentence must contain at least one independent clause.

EXERCISE 11A

Change each of the following fragments into a complete sentence.

1. Knowing her way around the city.

_____

_____

2. Ever since Johnny left.

_____

_____

3. Because the score was tied.

_____

_____

4. The smartest person in the class being the girl in the back row.

_____

_____

5. The two cars racing each other down the street.

_____

_____

6. If you know the answer.

_____

_____

7. The windows broken in the blast.

_____

_____

8. After the restaurant closed.

_____

_____

9. The dresses decorated with embroidery.

_____

_____

10. The pressure of winning the game and the fear of losing the tournament.

_____

_____

11. A quiet evening of intelligent conversation over a delicious dinner.

_____

_____

12. Thrilled with the chance of a promotion.

_____

_____

EXERCISE 11B

Correct any fragments that you find in the following exercise. If an item contains no fragments, label it *C* for *correct*.

1. Pipe organs have been found in most European churches for centuries.

2. As church music flowered during the Renaissance. The pipe organs grew in size and musical range.

3. Some churches were designed around the organ. So that it occupied a central place at the rear of the church or even over the altar.

4. For many tourists visiting Europe. The recitals on these pipe organs are a major attraction.

5. Because of electronic developments in the past century, many churches have switched from the old, expensive hand-built organs. To cheaper mass-produced electronic organs.

6. But the delicate mechanisms of electronic organs have proven vulnerable to a number of problems. Like air pollution.

7. In contrast, most of the older traditional pipe organs have worked for centuries with only minor repairs.

8. Also many of the great organists prefer the tone and touch of the old type of instrument.

9. In the past forty years, a revival of interest in the older pipe organs has taken place. Causing many young people to learn to build and restore them.

10. Quite a few American churches have purchased very old pipe organs that were abandoned years ago. And had them rebuilt. To give centuries more of service.

EXERCISE 11C

Many fragments would make sense if they were attached to the independent clause that precedes or follows them. In the following sets of three clauses, the middle clause is a fragment. Correct each fragment by attaching it either to the clause that precedes it or to the clause that follows it.

1. Rosa left the game early. Because she had a date. Her team won anyway.

2. Rosa left the game early. Because they played at the top of their form. Her team won anyway.

3. Rosa left the game early. As she felt sure of her team's victory. They lost in the top of the ninth inning.

4. The coach made the team very angry. When they arrived at practice the following day. Anger can inspire some teams.

5. Many smokers believe that smoking is unhealthy. Although they hold this belief. They continue to smoke.

6. It was the last thing we were expecting. Since we had never had a heat wave in October. We must have made the weather gods angry.

Compound and Complex Sentences
Versus Run-On Sentences and Fragments
Unit Review

Correct any sentence fragments, run-on sentences, or comma splices that you find in the following essay.

As the world faces increasing shortages of raw materials. New sources for products must be invented or discovered. One promising new source for many needs is the plant called *jojoba*. And pronounced as "ho-ho-ba."

Jojoba is an evergreen shrub, it grows naturally in northwestern Mexico and in some parts of Arizona and southern California. Because its root system may go 35 feet deep and because the jojoba has such thick, leathery leaves. It will grow in places too hot and dry for most other plants. It can go several years with no water, it can live in temperatures over 120° Fahrenheit.

The valuable part of the jojoba is the bean. Produced by the female plant. In the wild a female jojoba may produce from three to twenty pounds of seeds per year. Researchers in Illinois, California, and Israel have studied the jojoba as a farm crop, they believe it will yield from ten to twenty pounds per plant under cultivation. If the plant is irrigated by the new drip techniques. Once in production after the fourth year, the plant may continue to produce for over one hundred years.

Because it has some remarkable chemical properties. The wax from the jojoba bean has a variety of promising uses. It is already being used as an anti-foaming agent in the production of antibiotics. It has excellent qualities as a food stabilizer in products like mayonnaise it also works very well as a coating for fresh fruit.

In cosmetics jojoba oil is the "wettest" oil base ever discovered. Because it lacks the fishy odor of traditional oil bases. It is preferred by most manufacturers. But many cosmetic producers have had to give up advertising jojoba oil products. Since they cannot be produced yet in sufficient supply.

Jojoba oil may be the best lubricant ever discovered, it does not thin out at high temperatures. It also has an extraordinarily high flash point, and it has a shear factor exceeding all fossil fuels. Mobil Oil stated as far back as 1978 that it could use 10 million pounds per year for transmission fluid alone.

The market for this amazing oil from a little-known plant is there for those who are willing to gamble their dollars and their time as jojoba farmers.

Punctuation

12 Parenthetical Expressions

When speaking, people often interrupt their sentences with expressions such as *by the way, after all,* or *as a matter of fact.* These expressions are not really part of the main idea of the sentence; instead, they are interrupting — or **parenthetical** — expressions which speakers use to fill in the pauses while they are thinking of what to say next. In speech, people indicate that these parenthetical expressions are not part of the main idea of the sentence by pausing and dropping their voices before and after the expression. In writing, the same pauses are indicated with commas.

You have already learned that commas may be used to separate the clauses in compound and complex sentences. Another major function of the comma is to set off interrupting, or **parenthetical, expressions** from the rest of the sentence in which they occur.

Read the following sentences aloud, and notice how the commas around the italicized parenthetical expressions correspond to the pauses you make in speech.

Well, we've missed the bus again.
This is, *in fact,* the third time we've missed the bus this week.
We're going to be on time tomorrow, *I hope.*

The rule for punctuating parenthetical expressions is very simple:

A parenthetical expression must be completely set off from the rest of the sentence by commas.

This means that if the parenthetical expression occurs at the *beginning* of the sentence, it is *followed* by a comma. For example:

No, I do not want to hear that joke again.

If the parenthetical expression is at the *end* of the sentence, it is *preceded* by a comma.

Dallas is a nice place to live, *on the whole*.

If the parenthetical expression is in the *middle* of the sentence, it is both *preceded* and *followed* by a comma.

Koalas and kangaroos, *for example,* are both natives of Australia.

There are many parenthetical expressions. Some of the most frequently used ones are listed below.

after all
as a matter of fact
at any rate
etc. (an abbreviation of the Latin words *et cetera,* meaning ''and other things'')
for example
for instance
however
in fact
nevertheless
of course
on the other hand
on the whole
therefore
well (at the beginning of a sentence)
yes and *no* (at the beginning of a sentence)

Expressions such as the following are often parenthetical if they occur in a position *other than* at the beginning of a sentence:

doesn't it
I believe
I suppose
I think
isn't it
that is
you know

For example:

It's going to rain today, *isn't it?*
Tomorrow, *you know*, is our parents' anniversary.

Continual repetition of the parenthetical expression *you know* should be avoided in both speech and writing. If you are speaking clearly and your listener is paying attention, he knows what you are saying and does not have to be constantly reminded of the fact. Besides, you know, continually repeating *you know* can be irritating to your listener; and, you know, it doesn't really accomplish anything.

Study the following points carefully.

1. Some of the above words and phrases can be either parenthetical or not parenthetical, depending upon how they are used in a sentence. **If an expression is parenthetical, it can be removed from the sentence, and the remaining words will still be a complete sentence.**

    PARENTHETICAL An editorial is, *after all,* only one opinion about the news.
    NOT PARENTHETICAL Dinner was served *after all* of the guests had arrived.
    PARENTHETICAL Poodles are very intelligent dogs, *I think*.
    NOT PARENTHETICAL Sometimes *I think* about my childhood.

2. Since the abbreviation *etc.* is parenthetical, it must be *preceded* and *followed* by a comma if it occurs in the middle of a sentence.

    Shirts, ties, shaving lotion, *etc.,* are typical Father's Day gifts.

The final comma after *etc.* indicates that *etc.* is parenthetical. Notice that this comma serves a different function from the commas that separate the items in the series.

3. Some parenthetical expressions, like *however* and *nevertheless,* frequently join the clauses in a compound sentence. They should be punctuated as follows:

    The car has been repaired four times; *however,* it still doesn't run properly.
    The critics liked the new television series; *nevertheless,* the network cancelled the program.

The semicolon is needed because the clauses in the compound sentence are not joined by a coordinating conjunction (p. 85). The semicolon also takes the place of the comma that would normally precede a parenthetical expression occurring in the middle of a sentence. A comma follows the parenthetical expression to set it off from the remainder of the sentence.

4. People's names and titles are also set off by commas **if you are speaking directly to them** in a sentence. This type of construction is called **direct address**. The punctuation of direct address is the same as that used for parenthetical expressions.

    Ladies and gentlemen, the meeting is about to begin.
    Is it true, *Mr. Rossi,* that you plan to run for mayor?
    Are you coming to the party tonight, *Susan?*

Notice that names and titles are set off by commas only when the person is being *directly addressed* in the sentence. Otherwise, no commas are needed.

    My brother's name is Michael. (no comma)
    Michael, I need to borrow your car. (direct address)
    Dr. Howard will see you in her office. (no comma)
    Have you seen the X-rays yet, *Dr. Howard?* (direct address)

EXERCISE 12A

Part One Add commas to the following sentences wherever they are necessary. If a sentence needs no additional punctuation, label it *C* for *correct*. The sentences in this section of the exercise deal only with the punctuation of parenthetical expressions.

1. Most languages seem very different from one another don't they?

2. After all they have different alphabets, different sounds, and different systems of grammar.

3. Some linguistic scholars however believe in a universal grammar for all human languages.

4. This universal grammar has in fact never been discovered.

5. Nevertheless these scholars continue the search to prove its existence.

Part Two Add commas and semicolons to the following sentences wherever they are necessary. If a sentence needs no additional punctuation, label it *C* for *correct*. This section covers the punctuation of compound and complex sentences as well as parenthetical expressions and direct address.

6. Many inventors would like to become wealthy nevertheless a good invention by itself does not always make lots of money for its creator.

7. Some inventors are very creative but their lack of business skills causes them to fail in marketing their inventions.

8. The creator of the Moog Synthesizer for example had to sell his rights to the invention for his own attempts to market it were unsuccessful.

9. The company that purchased the rights to Moog's invention however has done very well with it.

10. On the other hand some inexperienced inventors are unable to protect the rights to their inventions because they do not know how to use the patent system.

11. Many inventors are reluctant to seek the services of a good patent attorney therefore they must later spend many costly years in court suing to recover damages.

12. The inventor of a special wrench finally won a suit against a company that had made millions from his invention however in order to secure his patent and recover damages, he had to go through fourteen years of court trials and spend much money for lawyers.

13. The richest inventors are more than just good inventors aren't they?

EXERCISE 12B

Add commas and semicolons to the following sentences wherever they are necessary. If a sentence needs no additional punctuation, label it *C* for *correct*. This exercise covers the punctuation of compound and complex sentences and parenthetical expressions.

1. Computers are man's most amazing machines; however, they have the built-in limitations of all machines.

2. Many machines are superhuman; one bulldozer, for example, can do the work of hundreds of men digging with their hands.

3. However, computers are the first machines to challenge the *mental* abilities of humans.

4. These machines have shown, haven't they, that they can remember more data and can solve longer problems than the smartest human.

5. Some people would say, I suppose, that computers can even talk like humans.

6. As a matter of fact, computers have an extremely low level of language ability, and it's not likely to get much better.

7. Word processors and computers may *seem* to talk like humans but so do juke boxes seem to make music.

8. Computers really act just like very complicated tape recorders; therefore, they are not using language the way we do at all.

9. In *2001: A Space Odyssey,* the computer HAL was given the power to talk intelligently however this was pure fiction.

10. Many computer scientists believe that no computer will ever "learn" a natural language like English or Spanish.

11. Could a computer after all know the subtle difference between *female parent* and *mother?*

12. On the other hand any three-year-old human can talk in a natural language with ease.

13. Well computers are only machines.

14. That's comforting isn't it?

EXERCISE 12C

Add commas and semicolons to the following letter wherever they are necessary. This exercise covers the punctuation of compound and complex sentences and parenthetical expressions.

Dear Mr. Williams,

I would rather speak to you in person no one seems to answer your phone so I'm writing you this note.

I want to talk to you about your son. Reginald is sometimes quite destructive. Last month Reginald ran his bike into my favorite rose bush. I know Reginald is only eight years old but he should respect other people's property, shouldn't he?

Last week Reginald was out walking your Great Dane. Who should come driving up but my mother-in-law and that dog tried to leap in the window of her car. In fact I distinctly heard Reginald tell the dog to attack her. This hardly shows a neighborly spirit does it Mr. Williams?

The last straw came this morning. My son may be two years older than Reginald but he has a frail constitution. Boyd came limping into the house he had mud all over his clothes and a cut lip. He said

Reginald had given him "a karate lesson." I suppose you might think

this is all very humorous Mr. Williams but it's not funny at all to

Reginald's victims. Reginald will be my victim if I ever catch him.

Your neighbor,

Boyd Harkness, Senior

13 Appositives

In sentences you sometimes use a noun whose meaning may not be as clear to your reader as it is to you. For example, suppose that you write:

Tohui is the star attraction of Mexico City's zoo.

If you think that your reader may not know what Tohui is, you can add a phrase to your sentence to provide more information about Tohui.

Tohui, *a baby panda,* is the star attraction of Mexico City's zoo.

This kind of explanatory phrase is called an **appositive** (from the verb *to appose,* meaning "to place things beside each other"). An appositive is a phrase placed beside a noun in order to clarify that noun's meaning. Study the following sentences, in which the appositives have been italicized. Notice that each appositive *immediately follows the noun it describes.*

Prince William, *the son of Prince Charles and Princess Diana,* is second in line to the British throne.

The month of January is named after Janus, *the Roman god of beginnings and endings.*

Timbuktu, *a center of African culture during the Middle Ages,* is a city near the Niger River in Mali.

As you can see, appositives must be set off by commas from the rest of the sentence just as parenthetical expressions are. Appositives are considered *extra* elements in a sentence because they add additional information about a noun that has already been *specifically identified.* For example, in the first sentence above, even without the appositive "the son of Prince Charles and Princess Diana," you know which person is second in line to the British throne because he has already been specifically identified as *Prince William.* In the second sentence, even without the appositive "the Roman god of beginnings and endings," the person after whom the month of January is named has already been specifically identified as *Janus.* Similarly, in the third sentence, even without the appositive "a center of African culture during the Middle Ages," you know that the city near the Niger River in Mali is specifically *Timbuktu.*

Here is the rule for punctuating this kind of explanatory phrase or clause:

If a phrase or clause adds additional information about a noun that has already been specifically identified, that phrase or clause must be completely set off from the rest of the sentence by commas.

In this lesson, you will be dealing with appositives, which are phrases. In Lesson 14, you will be applying the same rule to clauses.

Specifically identified includes mentioning either a person's first or last name, or both, or using words such as "my oldest brother," "my ten o'clock class on Monday," or "my hometown." The nouns in these last three phrases are considered to be *specifically identified* because even though you have not mentioned your brother's name, you can have only one "oldest" brother. Similarly, only one specific class can be your "ten o'clock class on Monday," and only one specific town can be your "hometown." In other words, *specifically identified* means limiting the meaning of a general word like *town* to *one particular* town or limiting a general word like *class* to *one particular* class.

Underline the appositives in the following sentences, and then punctuate them. Remember that appositives *follow* the nouns that they describe.

My youngest daughter a high-school senior hopes to attend the University

of Michigan next fall.

I am having an exam Friday in my nine o'clock class History 101.

Spanish 2 my most difficult subject meets four days a week.

Have you ever visited my hometown Orlando, Florida?

Sea World a group of marine amusement parks is owned by the publisher of

this textbook.

Foreign visitors to the United States want to see the Grand Canyon Arizo-

na's most famous tourist attraction.

On the other hand, if a phrase is *necessary* to establish the specific identity of a noun, it is *not* set off by commas. Study the difference between the following pair of sentences.

The novel *Great Expectations* is considered by many critics to be Charles Dickens' greatest work. (No commas are used to set off *Great Expectations* because the title is necessary to identify which of Dickens' many novels is considered to be his greatest work.)
Charles Dickens' fourteenth novel, *Great Expectations,* is considered by many critics to be his greatest work. (Commas are used to set off *Great Expectations* because Dickens' greatest work has already been specifically identified as his *fourteenth novel.*)

Most single-word appositives are necessary to establish the specific identity of the nouns they follow and are, therefore, *not* set off by commas.

My cousin *Carol* lives in Waco, Texas.
The word *obese* means "fat."
Certain shades of the color *pink* are used in prisons because they have a calming effect on the inmates.

Underline the appositives in the following sentences, and then add commas wherever they are necessary. Some sentences may not require commas.

Bolivia is named after Simón Bolívar a leader of the struggle to free South America from Spanish rule.

Grenada a small country in the West Indies has cartoon characters from Walt Disney movies on some of its postage stamps.

The word *spaghetti* originally meant "little pieces of cord" in Italian.

Cottage cheese a standard diet food contains more calories per half cup than a medium-sized potato.

My brother Paul is the tallest person in my family.

EXERCISE 13A

Add commas to the following sentences wherever they are necessary.

1. Next year they are going to vacation in his birthplace, Los Angeles.

2. Her favorite teacher, Mr. Reynoso, teaches history and English.

3. My uncle Jack asked me to visit him.

4. The movie *Dr. Strangelove* is about a mad scientist.

5. She has worked hard for her present position, Shift Supervisor.

6. I hear that your younger brother, Tom, now has a new title, "attorney at law."

7. Rachel Carson, a writer of scientific treatises on biology and popular essays about the environment, took much English in college.

8. They did their trout fishing at Lake Conway, a small lake north of Walker Junction.

9. She studied the harp, a stringed instrument, and the French horn, a brass instrument.

EXERCISE 13B

Add commas and semicolons to the following sentences wherever they are necessary. If a sentence needs no additional punctuation, label it *C* for *correct*. This exercise covers punctuation rules from previous lessons as well as the punctuation of appositives.

1. Being left-handed used to be considered unlucky or evil in olden times.

2. Even today left-handers a minority of the population must put up with certain inconveniences and prejudices.

3. Some implements such as pencils or pliers work equally well with either hand.

4. But many devices including some essential ones like scissors and watches and calculators are designed to be easier for right-handers.

5. The tendency to blame left-handers for being different may decrease as left-handedness becomes better understood.

6. There is strong evidence to tie handedness to brain *dominance* the left side of the brain is dominant in most right-handers.

7. For left-handers the dominant side would be the right hemisphere of the brain.

8. The right side of the brain controls a special set of skills the spatial skills needed in the arts.

9. The left side controls a different set of skills the skills of language.

10. The right-side dominance in left-handers explains two interesting facts about them their high frequency of learning disorders and the high frequency of left-handed artists such as Leonardo da Vinci.

11. It now appears that the cause of left-handedness may be testosterone a hormone present in the brain before birth.

12. Males normally have far more testosterone than females as a result, two of every three left-handers are male.

13. Too much testosterone in the brain of the unborn child seems to make the right side of the brain dominant and therefore causes lefthandedness.

14. If this is true there is a final puzzle the excess of testosterone in only 10 percent of the population.

EXERCISE 13C

Add appositive phrases to the following sentences. If necessary, set off the appositives with commas. The first two sentences have been done as examples.

1. My uncle _____*Joseph*_____ visits us every Christmas.

2. My uncle Joseph _____*, a New Yorker,*_____ visits us every Christmas.

3. Our 1979 Ford Pinto _____ is up for sale.

4. The car _____ is up for sale.

5. The slang word _____ means "good."

6. The White House _____ is in Washington, D.C.

7. Burt Reynolds _____ has made over thirty movies.

8. Of all my brothers, my brother _____ has the best sense of humor.

9. The singer _____ has made many records.

10. Pac Man _____ is played around the world.

11. The number _____ is my lucky number.

12. My only sister _____ won the contest.

14 Restrictive and Nonrestrictive Clauses

In Lesson 13 you learned that if a phrase adds extra information about a noun that has already been specifically identified, that phrase (an **appositive**) must be set off by commas. For example:

> Galileo, *a seventeenth-century Italian astronomer,* was the first person to publish maps of the moon.

The appositive is set off by commas because the first person to publish maps of the moon has already been specifically identified as *Galileo*.

On the other hand, if a phrase is *necessary* to establish the specific identity of a noun, the phrase is *not* set off by commas.

> The play *Our Town* has been read by millions of American high-school students.

The phrase *Our Town* is not set off by commas because it is necessary to identify which specific play has been read by millions of American high-school students.

The same rule that applies to the punctuation of appositive phrases also applies to the punctuation of *clauses*. Read the following sentences, in which the dependent clauses have been italicized. Can you see why one sentence in each pair has commas while the other does not?

The woman *who is sitting at the head of this table* is the director of the project.

Elena Morales, *who is sitting at the head of this table,* is the director of the project.

A game *which was invented in the United States in 1891* is now played throughout the world.

Basketball, *which was invented in the United States in 1891,* is now played throughout the world.

In the first sentence of each pair, the dependent clause is necessary to establish the specific identity of the noun it follows. This type of clause is called a **restrictive clause** because it *restricts,* or limits, the meaning of the word it describes. For example, in the first sentence if the restrictive clause were removed, the sentence would read:

The woman is the director of the project.

The meaning of this sentence is unclear since there are millions of women in the world, and any one of them might be the director of the project. But when the clause is added to the sentence, the meaning of the general word *woman* is now *restricted,* or limited, to *one particular* woman — *the woman who is sitting at the head of this table*. Thus, the restrictive clause "who is sitting at the head of this table" establishes the specific identity of the word *woman*.

Similarly, in the third sentence, the clause "which was invented in the United States in 1891" identifies *which* game (of all possible games) is now played throughout the world. It restricts the general word *game* to *one particular* game — *the game which was invented in the United States in 1891*.

Since restrictive clauses are necessary to establish the specific identity of the nouns they describe, the following punctuation rule applies:

Restrictive clauses are *not* set off by commas.

In contrast, the clauses in the second and fourth sentences are *not* necessary to identify which particular woman is the director of the project or which particular game is now played throughout the world. In these sentences, the woman has already been specifically identified as *Elena Morales,* and the game has already been specifically identified as *basketball.* Since these clauses are *not* restrictive clauses, they are called **nonrestrictive clauses**. Nonrestrictive clauses merely add extra information about the nouns they describe. They serve the same function as appositives and are punctuated in the same way.

> **Nonrestrictive clauses must be completely set off from the rest of the sentence by commas.**

This means that if a nonrestrictive clause is at the *end* of a sentence, it will be *preceded* by a comma. If it is in the *middle* of a sentence, it will be both *preceded and followed* by a comma. (Like appositives, nonrestrictive clauses never occur at the beginning of a sentence since they must follow the noun that they describe.)

The restrictive and nonrestrictive clauses that you have been studying are called **adjective clauses** because, like adjectives, these clauses describe nouns. The words that most frequently introduce adjective clauses are:

that
which
who
whom
whose

Like all clauses, adjective clauses must contain both a subject and a verb. But notice that in adjective clauses *the word that introduces the clause may also be the subject of the clause.*

                                S   V
Athena is a restaurant *which serves Greek food.*

Or the clause may contain a separate subject:

                         S   V
The countries *that I visited on my trip* included England and France.

Adjective clauses, like adverb clauses (see Lesson 9), are used in **complex sentences**. Although these sentences may not seem to be complex at first glance, if you study the sentences above, you will see that each of them has two subjects and two verbs. Also, if the adjective clause, which is the **dependent clause,** is removed from the sentence, a complete independent clause remains.

	S V
INDEPENDENT CLAUSE	Athena is a restaurant.

	S V
DEPENDENT CLAUSE	which serves Greek food

	S V
INDEPENDENT CLAUSE	The countries included England and France.

	S V
DEPENDENT CLAUSE	that I visited on my trip

An adjective clause often occurs in the middle of a sentence since it must follow the noun it describes. When an adjective clause is in the middle of a sentence, part of the independent clause precedes it, and the rest of the independent clause follows it. For example:

S   S   V   V
Canada, *which is a bilingual country,* uses both English and French as

official languages.

S   S   V V
The book *that I need* is not in the library.

A sentence may contain more than one adjective clause. Each clause is punctuated separately. In the following sentence, the first adjective clause is *nonrestrictive* (with commas), and the second clause is *restrictive* (no commas).

Death Valley, *which is the lowest point in the United States,* has daytime temperatures *that sometimes reach 124 degrees.*

Underline every adjective clause in each of the following sentences, and circle the noun that it describes. Then decide which clauses are restrictive (and do *not* need commas) and which clauses are nonrestrictive (and do need commas). Add the appropriate punctuation.

Note: Although clauses beginning with *who, whom, whose,* or *which* may be either restrictive or nonrestrictive, clauses which begin with *that* are *always* restrictive.

Have you seen the magazine that I left here yesterday?

My mother who was an excellent cook never bothered to write down her

recipes.

The Chun King company which manufactures canned and frozen Chinese

food was started by an Italian-American from Minnesota.

John is a person whom almost everyone likes.

California's Agua Caliente Indians whose land includes part of the resort

town of Palm Springs are the richest Indian tribe in the United States.

Susan's husband who left the hospital yesterday sent a box of candy to the

nurses who had cared for him.

EXERCISE 14A

Add commas and semicolons to the following sentences wherever they are necessary. If a sentence needs no additional punctuation, label it *C* for *correct*. Underline the adjective clauses and circle the nouns they describe. This exercise covers all punctuation rules up to this point in the book.

1. Playing cards have a history that is long and fascinating.

2. A Chinese legend credits the invention of playing cards to a lady of the imperial court who was bored with nothing to do.

3. Another legend about the origin of cards gives the credit to a wealthy wife of India whose husband needed a game to cure him of continually pulling at his beard.

4. Some historians believe playing cards were brought to Europe by gypsies others believe cards may have come back to Europe from Asia Minor during the Crusades which took place in the late Middle Ages.

5. The oldest decks of cards that have survived in Asia and Europe do not look much like modern playing cards.

6. Old Chinese cards measured about 1½ inches × 5 inches, and ancient Korean cards which were made of oiled silk were ½ inch wide and up to 8 inches long!

7. The oldest European cards that have survived are seventeen cards now on display in the National Library in Paris.

8. These beautiful cards which were probably from a personal set especially made for King Charles VI in 1392 are hand painted on a golden field with a silver border.

9. During the fifteenth and sixteenth centuries, each region of Europe had different types of decks these various types of decks were designed for games that were favored in that region.

10. Decks varied in the number of cards from forty up to ninety-seven, and there were many variations in the names and numbers of different suits.

11. *Trappola* for example a favorite game in Renaissance Italy used a deck of thirty-six cards with four suits that were called "cups," "swords," "coins," and "batons."

12. The spread of the new printing presses in the fifteenth century made playing cards much cheaper and more available.

13. Though mass produced, the early decks of printed cards were works of art because the great engravers who felt they were pioneers in a new art form competed with one another to see whose cards would be regarded as the most beautiful.

14. Today's machine-perfect decks of fifty-two clubs, diamonds, hearts, and spades are descendants of some distinguished ancestors that now rest quietly in libraries and museums.

EXERCISE 14B

Add commas and semicolons to the following sentences wherever they are necessary. If a sentence needs no additional punctuation, label it *C* for *correct*. Underline the adjective clauses in these sentences, and circle the nouns they describe.

1. On summer evenings we would meet our girlfriends near the lake in Central Park which was only two blocks from my home in New York City.

2. One evening from across the lake we heard a bugle sounding "Taps."

3. As the last note faded in dusk, the bugler whose figure had been silhouetted by the final rays of the sun turned and trotted away into the darkness of the trees.

4. My friends and I sat silently awash in the mood that the bugler had created.

5. The following evening the figure of the bugler reappeared across the lake and played "Stardust" with a tone that would break your heart.

6. He played another song the next evening, and I who never liked mysteries nicknamed him "The Phantom Bugler."

7. We waited the next evening for his bugle then we split into two groups and raced around the lake to the spot where he stood near the trees.

8. But when our two groups came breathlessly together the bugler was gone.

9. On the next night we began to run around the lake the moment that he began to play.

10. We were only 40 yards from the bugler at the end of his song, but not one of us who chased him could catch up with him.

11. Every evening for the rest of the summer, we gave that phantom bugler across the lake the head start that we owed him.

12. Then we chased him until we lost him in the dark.

13. In spite of all the beauty and mystery the bugler brought to our lives that summer, he was someone whom we were never to see face to face.

EXERCISE 14C

Part One Construct complex sentences of your own using the words listed below to form *restrictive* clauses. Underline the adjective clause in each of your sentences, and circle the noun it describes.

1. that: _____

_____

2. who: _____

_____

3. which: _____

_____

4. whose: _____

_____

Part Two Construct complex sentences of your own using the words listed below to form *nonrestrictive* clauses. Underline the adjective clause in each of your sentences, and circle the noun it describes. Use appropriate punctuation.

5. which: _____

_____

6. who: _____

_____

7. whose: _____

_____

8. whom: _____

_____

Part Three Underline the adjective clauses in the following sentences, and circle the word which each clause describes. If the clause is nonrestrictive, add the necessary punctuation. If the clause is restrictive, the sentence needs no additional punctuation, so label it *C* for *correct*.

9. Until very recently, female professional athletes have not earned salaries or prizes that were comparable to those earned by male athletes.

10. The financial rewards for women athletes who participate in team sports are still pitifully low.

11. However, women are now making much higher earnings in individual sports like golf and tennis which lend themselves to star promotion and endorsements of equipment.

12. By challenging Billie Jean King who was then the leading women's tennis player to a highly publicized and televised match in the 1970s, a male named Bobby Riggs may be the best friend that women's sports ever had.

13. Riggs lost, but this match demonstrated the interest that the public has in women athletes.

14. Tennis player Chris Evert Lloyd has since been able to earn over $3,850,000 in prizes alone.

15. Martina Navratilova who emigrated to the U.S. from Czechoslovakia has career earnings in pro tennis that may soon top Lloyd's.

15 Items in a Series and Dates and Addresses

A **series** consists of *three or more* items. Commas are placed between each item in a series in order to separate the items from each other. The final comma before the conjunction is optional.

> *Pineapples, sugar cane,* and *coffee* are three of Hawaii's main crops.
>
> or
>
> *Pineapples, sugar cane* and *coffee* are three of Hawaii's main crops.

If *every* item in a series is joined by a conjunction (*and, or,* or *nor*), no commas are needed since the conjunctions keep the individual items separated. This type of construction is used only when the writer wishes to place particular emphasis on the number of items in the series.

> The price of your tour includes your *air fare* and your *hotels* and your *meals.*

If a date or an address consists of more than one item, a comma is used after each part of the date or the address, *including a comma after the last item.* (If the last item in the series is also the last word in the sentence, only a period follows it.) Notice that this punctuation rule differs from the rule used for punctuating an ordinary series.

February 12, 1809, was the birthday of Abraham Lincoln.

The name of a month and the number of the day (February 12) are considered a single item and are separated from the year by a comma. However, notice that a comma also *follows* 1809, which is the last item in the date.

The old Chisholm Trail from San Antonio, Texas, to Abilene, Kansas, was used to move cattle from the range to railroad depots.

Notice the commas after "Texas" and "Kansas." These commas are used in addition to the commas that separate the names of the cities from the names of the states.

If a date or an address consists of only a single item, no comma is necessary.

February 14 is Valentine's Day.

I have lived in both Michigan and California.

A comma is not used before a Zip Code number.

The mailing address for Hollywood is Los Angeles, California 90028.

Punctuate the following sentences:

The discovery of gold on January 24 1848 began the great California Gold Rush.

You may have French fries baked beans or coleslaw with your hamburger.

How can any diet exclude fats and starches and protein?

You can drive from Granville Ohio to Johnson City Tennessee in eight hours.

The angry child cried screamed and stamped his feet.

EXERCISE 15A

Add commas to the following sentences wherever they are needed. If a sentence needs no additional punctuation, label it *C* for *correct*. This exercise covers only the punctuation of items in a series and dates and addresses.

1. Contact sports include boxing football and wrestling.

2. That bus goes through Columbus Pittsburgh and Philadelphia.

3. Roger Wilson Jane Smith Paul Hildebrandt and Laura Jones are running in the election.

4. Her Siamese cat is interesting intelligent and independent. (Notice that adjectives, as well as nouns, can be used in a series.)

5. The driver raced up to the intersection jammed on his brakes and stopped just in time. (Verbs, as well as other parts of speech, such as adverbs, can also form a series.)

6. For dinner we had salad with dressing fish with sauce and ice cream with topping.

7. Maria danced energetically enthusiastically and gracefully.

8. They moved from Billings Montana to Taylors South Carolina.

9. Reynaldo was born on October 5 1963.

10. She had resided in the small town of Wynne Arkansas before she lived in Detroit.

11. Many models of the Ford Mustang and Chevrolet Corvette are treasured as collector's items.

12. He strolled down to the river across the bridge and into the woods.

EXERCISE 15B

Add commas and semicolons to the following sentences wherever they are needed. If a sentence needs no additional punctuation, label it *C* for *correct*. This exercise covers all the punctuation rules that you have studied thus far.

1. She lives at The Sea Breeze Apartments 902 Ocean Avenue Atlantic City New Jersey 10321.

2. They thought the meal cost too much but they agreed that it was well cooked well served and well coordinated with the entertainment.

3. The Dixons visited Tacoma Seattle and the Olympic Peninsula in Washington State.

4. John Lasker was born on New Year's Day 1900 and died on August 13 1982.

5. Peter Irene Patty and Henry laughed and laughed and laughed.

6. The Solby High School Band of Solby Colorado won its twelfth national prize on May 22 of this year.

7. The Jazz Ensemble of Boston gave concerts in Kansas City and Topeka.

8. Send inquiries answer forms and new orders to 136 Hilton Avenue Redlands CA 92373.

9. The first quarter the second quarter and the third quarter were full of exciting passing and running plays however the fourth quarter was a total bore.

10. Come to the Christmas party on the 22nd of December we'll see you on January 1 1983 if you can't make it on the 22nd.

Punctuation
Unit Review

Add commas and semicolons (no periods) to the following sentences wherever they are necessary.

In recent years, the rising cost of food the desire for self-sufficiency and the pleasure of eating fresh food have nearly tripled the number of home vegetable gardeners. Even many city-dwellers are growing their own greens. A vegetable garden is after all just a miniature farm and a good farm crop requires good seed good soil and good care.

Good seed is plentiful everywhere today. Farmers used to carefully save the seeds from the plants that produced the largest and best crops but nowadays excellent weed-free seed is available everywhere in nurseries at hardware stores in markets or from seed catalogs. Plant science has made modern seeds almost fool-proof yet gardeners can expect even further improvements in seeds with new gene-splicing techniques.

Soil must be of the right texture so that the young plant can grow through it and later gain support from it. Good soil must not only contain the necessary food for the particular plant that one wishes to grow but it must also be fine enough to permit the root hairs to reach that food. A soil that hardens into clumps after watering will only starve even the strongest young plants.

Good seeds in good soil still require the gardener's careful attention. A "green thumb" is really a love of growing plants. Most plants produce better if their natural food supply is increased with fertilizers that are carefully selected for individual plant varieties. Some plants must be periodically thinned and almost all vegetables require weeding so that water and valuable nutrients are not stolen.

The vegetable gardener's greatest vigilance however must be used to save his little food factory from the plant kingdom's number one enemy bugs! Most home gardens are not in greenhouses away from the assaults of bugs so there are certain precautions that should be taken with outdoor gardens at home. Some plants such as peppers will protect other plants in their neighborhood from bugs. Or plants can be sprayed with insecticides before the bugs attack. Once the plant or fruit has already suffered a bug attack the gardener's best tactic is to identify the bug and find a specific remedy for it. This kind of knowledge may come only after several seasons of gardening.

A beginner who starts a small vegetable garden and follows the basic principles about seed soil and care may find his thumb is greener than he supposed. And even his mistakes may be edible.

[Handwritten notes:]

subjects	Objects
I we	me, us
you you	you, you
he, she, it they	him, her, it them
who	whom

the different between who & whom; who is subject of the sentence; whom is object.

UNIT FIVE

Pronoun Usage

16 Subject, Object, and Possessive Pronouns

[Handwritten notes:]

EX: Who hit the ball?

obj: Whom did the ball hit?   The ball did hit whom?

The ball was hit to whom?   Whom was the ball hit to?

Pronouns are words that are used to refer to persons, places, things, and ideas without repeating their names. In other words, pronouns are used in place of nouns. For example, rather than saying "Mark bought a new pen only yester-day, but Mark has already lost the pen," you can say, "Mark bought a new pen only yesterday, but *he* has already lost *it*." In this sentence, the pronoun *he* replaces *Mark,* and the pronoun *it* replaces *pen.* The noun that the pronoun replaces is called the **antecedent** (Latin for "to go before") of the pronoun.

There are several different kinds of pronouns, but in this lesson you will be studying only **subject pronouns, object pronouns,** and **possessive pronouns.**

Singular Pronouns	*Subject*	*Object*	*Possessive*
	I	me	my, mine
	you	you	your, yours
	he	him	his
	she	her	her, hers
	it	it	its

[Handwritten notes:]

The man (who lives there) is not home.

The man (whom you seek) is not home.

The man (to whom you spoke) is not home.

connect with man

165

Plural Pronouns	*Subject*	*Object*	*Possessive*
	we	us	our, ours
	you	you	your, yours
	they	them	their, theirs

As their name suggests, **subject pronouns** are used as the *subject* of a sentence or a clause. For example:

She is an electrical engineer at IBM.
They own the house on the corner.

In *formal* speech and writing, subject pronouns are also used after forms of the verb *be,* as in:

That is *he* at the door.
It is *I.*
If I were *she,* I'd take the job.

In formal speech and writing, subject pronouns are used after forms of the verb *be* because they refer to the *same* thing or person as the subject.

That = *he* at the door.
It = *I.*
If I = *she,* I'd take the job.

However, in *informal* speech, many people would use object pronouns in the sentences below.

That is (or *That's*) *him* at the door.
It is (or *It's*) *me.*
If I were *her,* I'd take the job.

Whether you choose to say "it is I" or "it is me" depends upon the circumstances. If you are taking an English test or writing a formal essay, using subject pronouns after forms of *be* is appropriate and expected. But if you are speaking casually with a friend, "it is I" may sound artificial, and the informal "it is me" might be more suitable.

The way in which words and phrases are *actually* used by most people in various situations is called **usage**. In the past, some educated people always used very formal English. Nowadays, however, people are expected to use the type of language that is suitable for a given situation. It is as inappropriate to use very formal language in an informal situation, such as a casual conversation with a close friend, as it is to use informal language, for example slang, in a formal essay.

In this unit, you will be studying both grammar and usage. Try to keep clear in your mind those situations in which you have a choice between formal and informal constructions (usage) and those situations in which only one pronoun form is correct at all times (grammar).

"It is *she*" versus "It is *her*" = usage.
"*I* am here" versus "*Me* am here" = grammar.

Object pronouns are used as objects of prepositions, as direct objects, and as indirect objects.

You will remember that the noun or pronoun in a prepositional phrase is called the **object of the preposition.** That is why an object pronoun replaces the noun. For example:

The dog barked at *Helen*.
The dog barked at *her*.
The professor spoke to the *students*.
The professor spoke to *them*.

Object pronouns are also used as direct objects. A **direct object** is the word that *receives* the action of the verb, as opposed to the subject, which *performs* the action of the verb.

The doctor examined the *patients*.
   (subject)   (direct object)

The doctor examined *them*.

I met *Paul* a year ago.
(subject) (direct object)

I met *him* a year ago.

Another way in which object pronouns are used is as indirect objects. An **indirect object** is the person or thing *to whom* or *for whom* something is done.

We gave the *bride* a gift.
(subject)   (indirect (direct
                object) object)

We gave *her* a gift.

The previous sentence is another way of saying, "We gave a gift *to her.*"

Gene bought his *son* a bicycle.
(subject)   (indirect (direct
                object) object)

Gene bought *him* a bicycle.

The previous sentence is another way of saying, "Gene bought a bicycle *for him.*"

Possessive pronouns are used to show ownership.
The supermarket raised *its* prices.
The students buy *their* books at the campus bookstore.

Very few people make pronoun errors when there is only one subject or one object in a sentence. For example, no native speaker of English would say, "Me am here" instead of "I am here." However, people often do make mistakes when two subjects or two objects follow each other in a sentence. For example, which of the following two sentences is grammatically correct?

Mrs. Jones invited my husband and *me* to her party.
Mrs. Jones invited my husband and *I* to her party.

To determine the correct pronoun in this kind of "double" construction, split the sentence in two like this:

1. Mrs. Jones invited my husband to her party.
2. Mrs. Jones invited (me, I) to her party.

As you can tell after you have split the sentence in two, it would be incorrect to say "Mrs. Jones invited *I* to her party." The correct pronoun is *me,* which is the direct object of the verb *invited.* Therefore, the whole sentence should read:

Mrs. Jones invited my husband and *me* to her party.

Which of the following two sentences is correct?

Carla showed Betty and *I* her snapshots.
Carla showed Betty and *me* her snapshots.

Again, split the sentences in two.

1. Carla showed Betty her snapshots.
2. Carla showed (I, me) her snapshots.

Now, which pronoun is correct?

Another very common pronoun error is using subject pronouns instead of object pronouns after prepositions. The object of a preposition must be an *object* pronoun. Which of the following two sentences is correct?

The waiter handed menus to Larry and *I.*
The waiter handed menus to Larry and *me.*

If you split the sentence in two, you have:

1. The waiter handed menus to Larry.
2. The waiter handed menus to (I, me).

The correct pronoun is *me,* which is the object of the preposition *to.* Therefore, the correct sentence is:

The waiter handed menus to Larry and *me.*

It is extremely important that you do not decide which pronoun to use simply on the basis of what "sounds better" *unless you split the sentence in two first.* To many people, "Mrs. Jones invited my husband and *I* to her party" sounds more "correct" than "Mrs. Jones invited my husband and *me* to her party"; yet, as you have seen, *me* is actually the correct pronoun.

Another example of choosing an incorrect pronoun because it "sounds better" is the frequent misuse of the subject pronoun *I* after the preposition *between*. As you already know, the object of a preposition must be an *object* pronoun. Therefore, it is always incorrect to say "between you and *I*." The *correct* construction is "between you and *me*."

Circle the pronoun that correctly completes each of the following sentences.

My sister and (he, him) work for the same company.

The candy is for you and (she, her).

The landlord gave my roommate and (I, me) a rent increase notice.

The new fence cost our neighbors and (we, us) three hundred dollars.

This is a secret between you and (I, me).

Occasionally you may use constructions like the following:

We citizens must participate in politics.
Is the change in graduation requirements going to affect *us seniors*?

To determine whether the sentence requires a subject or an object pronoun, see which pronoun would be correct if the pronoun appeared in the sentence by itself rather than being followed by a noun.

(We, Us) citizens must participate in politics. =
(We, Us) must participate in politics.

Is the change in graduation requirements going to affect (we, us) seniors?
=
Is the change in graduation requirements going to affect (we, us)?

The correct pronouns are *We* citizens and *us* seniors.

Circle the pronoun that correctly completes each of the following sentences.

It is up to (we, us) neighbors to ask the city to install more street lights.

(We, Us) parents should show an interest in our children's schoolwork.

EXERCISE 16A

The first part of this exercise is intended for a quick review of subject and object pronouns. Reverse each sentence so that the subject pronoun becomes the object and the object pronoun becomes the subject.

Example: *I* waited for *them*.
Answer: *They* waited for *me*.

1. *He* called *her* yesterday.

2. *They* liked *me* very much.

3. *She* washed the car for *him* on Friday.

4. *I* wrote *them* frequently.

5. *He* did see *you* in the dark.

6. *We* depended on *her* for entertainment.

7. *She* is like sunshine to *him*.

8. *They* gave *us* three free passes.

Circle the pronoun that correctly completes each sentence. Remember to split the sentence if it contains a "double" construction. Apply the rules of formal English usage.

9. Thomas and (he, him) were roommates.

10. It was (she, her) who won the prize.

11. You and (he, him) should go to the party together.

12. Mary and (they, them) went to the market.

13. Is it (he, him) at the door?

14. Jack and (me, I) have the same birthday.

15. The question must be decided by (us, we) family members.

16. Can you tell who voted for Sue and (he, him)?

17. The committee will split the fifty dollars between you and (I, me).

18. Everyone is proud of (they, them) and their award.

19. (We, Us) fans must get behind our team.

20. Why not split the cake between Joe and (she, her)?

INPUT Name, $, $ to bet.
  Choose dealer.
  Dealer first.
  → player

  Throw dices.
    show dice # show
    (1.2.3.4.5.6)
memo dealer's #.
  compare with dealer
  decide win or lose $

EXERCISE 16B

Some of the following sentences contain pronoun errors. Cross out the incorrect pronouns, and write in the correct forms. If a sentence contains no pronoun errors, label it *C* for *correct*. Apply the rules of formal English usage.

1. Don't count on Jack and I to help.

2. We students will succeed in the course.

3. Each spring my grandfather and me go to the lake.

4. You and him have won a new radio.

5. With her and me on your side, victory is certain.

6. The dog ran through the woods looking for Dan and I.

7. She always writes my mom and I at Christmas.

8. Us girls in the band have new uniforms.

9. You could please him and his wife by going to the party.

10. Can you save seats for Sheryl and me?

11. If us party members don't vote, who will?

12. They required both John and her to sign the form.

13. The chairman wishes to speak for us delegates.

14. Both his cousin and him have hiked that trail.

15. The first winners to reach the microphone were the Smiths and us.

16. Irene and them were sure to come in first.

17. I haven't noticed Maria with her in this place.

18. Our relatives and us are opening a restaurant.

19. Just between you and I, can we support that proposed law?

20. They asked Lonnie and I to take care of their lawn.

EXERCISE 16C

Part One Give the following sentences two subjects by adding a subject pronoun to each sentence. *Use a different pronoun for each sentence.* Apply the rules of formal English usage. The first sentence has been done as an example.

         and he
1. George ∧ worked for the Air Force.

2. The woman upstairs went downtown early.

3. My boss enjoyed the movie.

4. The man in the truck had a collision.

5. The band got along well together.

6. That man on the beach jogged every morning.

7. Those people knew each other a long time ago.

Part Two Give the following sentences two objects by adding an object pronoun to each sentence. *Use a different object pronoun for each sentence.* Apply the rules of formal English usage. The first sentence has been done as an example.

         and me
8. She sent Mary ∧ a present.

9. I called Sam yesterday.

10. Rose sang to Raul.

11. The meal was prepared for my brother.

12. She drives with Marlene.

13. I have known you a long time.

14. Call Lester.

17 Pronouns in Comparisons and Pronouns with -self, -selves

Using Pronouns in Comparisons

In speech and in writing, we often compare two people or two things with each other. For example:

Judy is younger than *I* am.
The dentist charged *Ellen* more than he charged *me*.

In the sentences above, it is easy to tell whether a subject pronoun or an object pronoun should be used in each comparison. In the first sentence, the subject pronoun *I* is correct because it would be clearly ungrammatical to say that "Judy is younger than *me* am." In the second sentence, the object pronoun *me* is correct because you would not say that "The dentist charged Ellen more than he charged *I*."

However, people usually do not write out their comparisons completely. They use a shortened form instead. For example:

Joel swims better than *I*.
The news surprised *Gordon* more than *me*.

In these cases, it is possible to determine which pronoun is correct by mentally filling in the words that have been left out of the comparison.

Joel swims better than I (do).
The news surprised Gordon more than (it surprised) me.

Fill in the missing words to determine which pronouns are correct in the following sentences.

My sister earns more money than (I, me).

Speaking in public is easier for Maria than (I, me).

Our neighbors water the lawn more than (we, us).

The earthquake scared you more than (she, her).

When you fill in the missing words, the correct comparisons are:

My sister earns more money than *I* (do).
Speaking in public is easier for Maria than (it is for) *me*.
Our neighbors water the lawn more than *we* (do).
The earthquake scared you more than (it scared) *her*.

In *informal* usage, you often hear people use object pronouns instead of subject pronouns in comparisons. (For example, ''He's taller than me'' instead of ''He's taller than I.'') However, these forms are generally considered inappropriate in writing and formal speech. You should be especially careful in situations where the wrong pronoun can change the meaning of the entire sentence. For example, ''Mary danced with George more than *I* (danced with him)'' does not mean the same thing as ''Mary danced with George more than (she danced with) *me*.'' In addition, using the wrong pronoun can sometimes lead to unintentionally ridiculous sentences, such as:

My girlfriend likes pizza more than me.

Unless your girlfriend happens to like food more than she likes you, the correct pronoun would be:

My girlfriend likes pizza more than *I* (do).

(Note: The conjunction *than,* which is used in comparisons, should not be confused with the adverb *then.*)

Avoiding Doubled Subjects

Do not "double," or repeat, the subject of a sentence by repeating the noun in its pronoun form.

INCORRECT   My roommate, he never pays his share of the phone bill.
CORRECT   My roommate never pays his share of the phone bill.
INCORRECT   Those children, they can be pests sometimes.
CORRECT   Those children can be pests sometimes.

Pronouns with -self, -selves

Some pronouns end in *-self* or *-selves:*

Singular	*Plural*
myself	ourselves
yourself	yourselves
himself	themselves
herself	
itself	

These pronouns can be used in two ways. They can be reflexive pronouns. **Reflexive pronouns** are used when the object of the verb or the object of the preposition is the same person or thing as the subject. For example:

I hurt *myself.* (myself = I)
Lisa supports *herself.* (herself = Lisa)
Al often talks to *himself.* (himself = Al)

Or they may be used for *emphasis.*

The professor *himself* said that this quiz wouldn't count.
Did you eat that entire pizza *yourself?*
We painted our house *ourselves.*

Notice that the singular forms of reflexive pronouns end in *self,* and the plural forms end in *selves*. In standard English, there are no such forms as *hisself, ourselfs, theirselfs,* or *themselfs*. These forms are considered nonstandard in both speech and writing and should be avoided unless you are using a dialect in which they are the customary forms.

In formal English, the reflexive pronoun *myself* is not used in place of a subject or an object pronoun.

INCORRECT	Pam and *myself* would like to invite you to dinner.
CORRECT	Pam and *I* would like to invite you to dinner.
INCORRECT	This gift is from Tom and *myself*.
CORRECT	This gift is from Tom and *me*.

Myself is sometimes used as a subject or an object pronoun in informal usage, but even in these cases the use of the correct subject or object pronoun is preferred. Referring to yourself as *myself* rather than as *I* or *me* does *not* make you sound more polite or more modest.

EXERCISE 17A

Circle the pronoun that most logically and correctly completes each sentence. Apply the rules of formal English usage.

1. She was sitting there longer than (he, him).

2. Tom and (I, myself) were last in line.

3. The police talked to the people next door and (us, we).

4. The coach liked you more than (they, them) because you try harder.

5. That hair style flatters her more than (I, me).

6. Are they going to fix dinner all by (theirselfs, themselves)?

7. The boss asked John and (myself, me) to come in early.

8. The happiest people at the fiesta were Lupe and (I, me).

9. I have been in the club longer than (he, him).

10. The sheriff gave Harry a sterner warning than (she, her).

11. They speak poorer Spanish than (we, us).

12. Send the pack to my uncle or (me, myself).

13. Though they both like that kind of chocolate cake, she ate twice as much as (him, he).

14. Either Tony or (I, me) will pick you up.

15. Are Karen and (them, they) neighbors?

EXERCISE 17B

If a sentence contains a pronoun error, cross out the incorrect pronoun, and write in the correct form. If a sentence has a "doubled subject," correct this mistake. If the sentence contains no pronoun errors, label it *C* for *correct*. Apply the rules of formal English usage.

1. I don't believe either you or him is right.

2. Can she answer the phone, or will she want you and I to stay?

3. He is certainly fooling hisself when he lies to people.

4. That girl, she just gets stronger and stronger.

5. Give the book to Michael or myself after the exam.

6. Although your name was not on the program, you deserve as much credit as us.

7. It couldn't have been he who told you that story.

8. Why doesn't Mom split the chores between you and I?

9. Even though Russell tries to be fair to both of us, isn't he easier on you than me?

10. It's hard to say whether Mary or I am the better player.

11. Rock concerts appeal to Rosa more than me.

12. The Williams, they have a new pickup.

13. Can't you and them agree on the menu?

14. Ike needs you and I to help him move the sofa.

15. She ate more than he.

18 Agreement of Pronouns with Their Antecedents

Agreement in Number

Like nouns, pronouns may be either singular or plural, depending upon whether they refer to one or to more than one person or thing. Following are the subject, object, and possessive pronouns you have learned, divided into singular and plural categories.

Singular Pronouns	*Subject*	*Object*	*Possessive*
	I	me	my, mine
	you	you	your, yours
	he	him	his
	she	her	her, hers
	it	it	its

Plural Pronouns	*Subject*	*Object*	*Possessive*
	we	us	our, ours
	you	you	your, yours
	they	them	their, theirs

Just as a subject must agree in number with its verb, a pronoun must agree in number with its **antecedent.** (The antecedent, you will remember, is the noun to which the pronoun refers.) In other words, if the antecedent is *singular,* the pronoun must be *singular.* If the antecedent is *plural,* the pronoun must be *plural.*

Study the following sentences, in which both the pronouns and their antecedents have been italicized.

Because the *man* had been badly injured in the accident, *he* was taken to a hospital.

Because the *men* had been badly injured in the accident, *they* were taken to a hospital.

Obviously, few people would make pronoun agreement errors in the above sentences since *man* is clearly singular, and *men* is clearly plural. However, people often make pronoun agreement errors in cases like the following:

INCORRECT   Every airline *passenger* should buckle *their* seatbelt before the plane takes off.

CORRECT   Every airline *passenger* should buckle *his* seatbelt before the plane takes off.

Since airline passengers include females as well as males, it would be equally correct to say:

Every airline passenger should buckle *her* seatbelt before the plane takes off.

or

Every airline passenger should buckle *his or her* seatbelt before the plane takes off.

For a more detailed discussion of the *his or her* construction, see the section on "Avoiding Sexist Language" on page 188.

INCORRECT   Every working person must have *their* own Social Security card.

CORRECT   Every working person must have *his* own Social Security card.

What causes people to make mistakes like these? The mistakes may occur because when a writer describes a *passenger,* he or she is thinking of passengers (plural) in general. Similarly, a writer may think of a *person* as people in general. Nevertheless, since *passenger* and *person* are singular nouns, they must be used with singular pronouns.

Notice that if several pronouns refer to the same antecedent, *all* of the pronouns must agree in number with that antecedent.

If *Frank* wants a raise in salary, *he* will have to improve *his* work.
Whenever my *neighbors* go on a vacation, *they* take *their* dogs with *them.*

Another common pronoun agreement error involves **indefinite pronouns.** As you learned in Lesson 5 on subject– verb agreement (p. 52), indefinite pronouns are *singular* and require *singular* verbs. (For example, "Everyone *is* here," *not* "Everyone *are* here.") Similarly, when indefinite pronouns are used as antecedents, they require *singular* subject, object, and possessive pronouns.

The following words are singular indefinite pronouns:

memorize

anybody, anyone, anything
each, each one
either, neither
everybody, everyone, everything
nobody, no one, nothing
somebody, someone, something

Notice the use of singular pronouns with these words.

Everyone did as she pleased.
Somebody has forgotten *her* shawl.
Either of the choices has *its* disadvantages.

In informal spoken English, plural pronouns are often used with indefinite pronoun antecedents. However, this construction is generally not considered appropriate in formal speech or writing.

INFORMAL   *Somebody* wants *their* husband to phone *them.*
FORMAL   *Somebody* wants *her* husband to phone *her.*

In some sentences, an indefinite pronoun is so clearly plural in meaning that a singular pronoun sounds awkward with it. For example:

Everyone on this block must be wealthy because *he* drives a Cadillac or a Continental.

In a case such as this, the sentence can be reworded.

All the *people* on this block must be wealthy because *they* all drive a Cadillac or a Continental.

Avoiding Sexist Language

Although the matching of singular pronouns with singular antecedents is a *grammatical* problem, a *usage* problem may occur if the antecedent of a singular pronoun refers to both sexes. In the past, singular masculine pronouns were used to refer to antecedents such as *person* or *passenger* even if these antecedents included women as well as men. Now, with the increased emphasis on the status of women in society, many writers prefer to use forms that include both sexes, such as *he or she* or *his or her*. For example:

Every *student* should turn *his or her* papers in on time.
If *anyone* has seen the missing child, *he or she* should call the police immediately.

Avoiding sexist language is a problem of usage, not of grammar. In order to simplify the rules for you while you are still studying grammar, most of the exercises in this unit will offer you the choice between one singular pronoun (either masculine or feminine) and one plural pronoun. For example:

Everyone should do (her, their) best on the job.
Each parent is responsible for (his, their) own children.

Which pronouns would be correct in the following sentences according to the rules of formal English usage?

If a person wants to lose weight, (he, they) should eat less and exercise more.

Each of the teams hopes to win (its, their) games.

Ballerinas have a difficult life because much of (her, their) time is spent traveling from city to city.

Somebody has parked (his, their) car in front of my driveway.

Neither of the professors met (her, their) classes today.

If somebody wants to say something (she, they) should speak up.

Agreement in Person

In grammar, pronouns are classified into groups called **persons. First person** refers to the person who is speaking. **Second person** is the person being spoken to. **Third person** is the person or thing being spoken about. Below is a chart of subject pronouns grouped according to person.

	Singular	*Plural*
first person	I	we
second person	you	you
third person	he, she, it	they

All nouns are considered third person (either singular or plural) because nouns can be replaced by third-person pronouns (for example, *Bob* = *he; a book* = *it; apples* = *they*).

Just as a pronoun and its antecedent must agree in number, they must also agree in person. Agreement in person usually becomes a problem only when the second-person pronoun *you* is incorrectly used with a third-person antecedent. Study the following examples.

INCORRECT   If *anyone* is drunk, *you* should not drive.
CORRECT   If *anyone* is drunk, *he* should not drive.
INCORRECT   When *drivers* change lanes, *you* should signal first.
CORRECT   When *drivers* change lanes, *they* should signal first.

This type of mistake is called a **shift in person** and is considered a serious grammatical error.

In addition to avoiding shifts in person within individual sentences, you should try to be consistent in your use of person when you are writing essays. In general, an entire essay is written in the same person. If, for example, you are writing an essay about the special problems faced by students who work full-time, you will probably use either the first or the third person. You should avoid shifts into the second person *(you)* since *you* refers to the reader of your paper and not to the students you are writing about.

INCORRECT   *Students* who work full-time often find it difficult to study. For example, *you* often come home from *your* job too exhausted to concentrate on *your* homework.

CORRECT   *Students* who work full-time often find it difficult to study. For example, *they* often come home from *their* job too exhausted to concentrate on *their* homework.

Circle the pronoun that correctly completes each sentence.

If a person wants to vote, (you, he, they) must register first.

Some states provide bilingual ballots for voters if (you, she, they) cannot

     read English.

Please be quiet; (your, his, their) talking is disturbing me.

EXERCISE 18A

Circle the pronouns that correctly complete each sentence. Apply the rules of formal English usage.

1. No one was as angry about the accident as (she, her).

2. (He, Him) and I had just finished the test before the bell rang.

3. Will you divide this between my cousin and (me, I)?

4. Neither of the teams has easy opponents on (their, its) schedule.

5. Has everyone filled (his, their) canteen?

6. If an employee at one of these levels is going to get a promotion, (she, they) will need to work harder.

7. Everyone in the class wants (his, their) voice heard.

8. Though I practice more than (she, her), I score fewer points.

9. When voters see the candidates, (you, they) will elect the best person.

10. I was finished much sooner than (them, they).

11. The union is run by the members (theirselves, themselves).

12. Because Joan and (she, her) joined the club at the same time, they have equal privileges.

13. Either the coach or the assistant coach will take you in (their, her) car.
   singular.

14. After a model gets on a magazine cover, (she, you) can earn thousands of dollars for each assignment.

15. She has defeated more opponents in open competition than (he, him).

16. The difference between Ron and (myself, me) is that he likes onions.

EXERCISE 18B

If a sentence contains an error in pronoun usage, cross out the incorrect pronoun, and write in the correct form. Some sentences contain more than one error. If a sentence contains no pronoun errors, label it *C* for *correct*. Apply the rules of formal English usage.

1. Somebody in the group left their shoes on the bus, didn't they?

2. After she cleaned the bike, she put a "For Sale" sign on it.

3. Mary was more upset than me.

4. After a homeowner receives one of these notices, they must pay a fine.

5. It was him and not his sister who answered correctly.

6. The game warden could see that Frank and I had this year's license.

7. All members must remember to report your activities.

8. Will someone lend George their textbook over the weekend?

9. Mary owns many more acres than us.

10. They had heard that Bill and him were elected co-captains.

11. When the fans were told about the changes in the program, they became angry.

12. Not one of the boys reported that their locker was safe.

13. They have only themselfs to blame.

14. Either Mark or Pete left their keys on the bench.

15. Can you leave early with the rest of the team and I?

16. His constant praise was very encouraging to Judy and me.

17. Anyone who doesn't go will be sorry they didn't.

EXERCISE 18C

Complete the following sentences by adding a pronoun. Be sure your choice of pronoun agrees in number with its antecedent. Apply the rules of formal English usage. The first sentence has been done as an example.

1. If anyone wishes to belong, _____*she*_____ must pay dues.

2. Jack is going to Wisconsin for _____ vacation.

3. Somebody has dropped _____ purse.

4. When taxpayers see waste in government, _____ get angry.

5. No one will pass Ms. Allen's P.E. class, if _____ doesn't try hard.

6. Although Irene and _____ have not always agreed, they do like each other.

7. Everyone in the room has _____ own solution to the problem.

8. Before a person visits the prison, _____ must undergo an inspection.

9. They go to more movies than _____.

10. In many countries, everyone must carry an identification card with _____ at all times.

11. Each girl on the team was asked to bring _____ own lunch.

12. Neither of the boys should be ashamed of _____ performance.

13. If you buy a guaranteed product nowadays, you should feel certain of _____ quality.

19 Order of Pronouns and Spelling of Possessives

Order of Pronouns

When you are referring to someone else and to yourself in the same sentence, mention the other person's name (or the pronoun that replaces the name) before you mention your own.

INCORRECT	*I* and *Don* attended the same high school
CORRECT	*Don* and *I* attended the same high school.
INCORRECT	You can buy the tickets from *me* or *him*.
CORRECT	You can buy the tickets from *him* or *me*.

This construction is actually not a rule of grammar; rather, it is considered a matter of courtesy.

Possessive Pronouns

Here is a list of possessive pronouns that you have already studied. This time, look carefully at how they are spelled and punctuated.

	Singular	*Plural*
first person	my, mine	our, ours
second person	your, yours	your, yours
third person	his	their, theirs
	her, hers	
	its	

Possessive pronouns do *not* contain apostrophes.

INCORRECT   The tennis racket is *their's*.
CORRECT   The tennis racket is *theirs*.

Be especially careful not to confuse the possessive pronoun *its* with the contraction *it's* (it is).

INCORRECT   The television series was cancelled because *it's* ratings were low.
CORRECT   The television series was cancelled because *its* ratings were low.

Also do not confuse the following pairs of words: *whose,* which is the possessive form of *who,* with *who's* (who is); *your,* which is the possessive form of *you,* with *you're* (you are); and *their,* which is the possessive form of *they,* with *they're* (they are).

Who's there? (Who is there?)
Whose book is this?
You're an excellent photographer.
Your car needs new tires.
They're ready to leave.
Their house was robbed.

Circle the pronoun that correctly completes each sentence.

This pen is (yours, your's).

(Whose, Who's) your doctor?

The store just raised (its, it's) prices.

I don't know (whose, who's) dog that is.

(Your, You're) subscription has expired.

The new car is (theirs, their's).

A final note: When you do pronoun exercises, or when you use pronouns in your own writing, remember to apply the rules. If you rely only on what "sounds right," your ear will usually supply only those pronouns that are appropriate in *informal* English.

EXERCISE 19A

If a sentence contains an error in pronoun usage, cross out the incorrect pronoun, and write in the correct form. Some sentences may contain more than one error. If a sentence contains no pronoun errors, label it *C* for *correct*. Apply the rules of formal English usage.

1. We team members participate in a year-round conditioning program.

2. Your not going to take physics this semester, are you?

you're

3. Don't save any seats for the girls and I. *me*

4. When you take the dog, don't forget it's leash. *its*

5. She wants to know whose leaving on the early bus. *who's*

6. The package was sent to me and Cristina.

7. Its not likely that the movie will live up to its publicity.

8. This raincoat is mine because your's has a rip in the collar.

9. Who's car is parked next to the red station wagon? *Whose*

10. Their always home on their day off. *They're*

11. If its all right with you, I would like to finish before it's dark. *it's*

12. Her father sent me and Raul to the store.

13. The request should always come from the manager on duty or myself. *me*

14. For that type of fishing, get a spinning reel because it's line won't get tangled.

EXERCISE 19B

If a sentence contains an error in pronoun usage, cross out the incorrect pronoun, and write in the correct form. Some sentences may contain more than one error. If a sentence contains no pronoun errors, label it *C* for *correct*. Apply the rules of formal English usage.

1. Has each of the students turned in their overdue books?

2. That radio isn't Billy's or your's.

3. Us neighbors should keep this to ourselves.

4. Whenever a radio station takes a station break, they should give the time of day if they wish to serve their listeners.

5. The practical joke was blamed on Donald and me.

6. Just between you and I, I wouldn't spend a cent in that coffee shop.

7. People without current memberships should turn in your club emblems.

8. Your only as old as you think you are.

9. If a person visits New York for the first time in their life, you should visit Radio City Music Hall.

10. Denver is a beautiful city, but it's altitude is too high for my uncle.

11. The difference between me and Richard is that I mean what I say.

12. Anybody who wants to pass Mr. Granatello's class must be on time and do their homework.

EXERCISE 19C

Part One   Construct sentences in which you use the possessive pronouns listed in Lesson 19 at the top of page 198. Use a different pronoun for each sentence. Be sure of the spelling of the pronoun.

1. _____

2. _____

3. _____

4. _____

5. _____

6. _____

7. _____

8. _____

9. _____

10. _____

11. _____

12. _____

13. _____

14. _____

Part Two   The pairs of words listed below are often confused because of their similarity in sound and spelling. Show that you understand the difference in meaning between the two words in each pair by constructing a sentence in which you use the word correctly.

who's   you're   they're
whose   your   their

1. _____

2. _____

3. _____

4. _____

5. _____

6. _____

Pronoun Usage
Unit Review

Part One Some of the following sentences contain pronoun errors. Cross out the incorrect pronouns, and write in the correct forms. If a sentence contains no pronoun errors, label it *C* for *correct*. Apply the rules of formal English usage.

1. After it's fur has been washed, Mike's dog sprays water everywhere.

2. My parents are going to paint their house themselfs.

3. If you're going to visit Disneyland, take your camera along.

4. Mr. Lopez asked me and my friend to go out for basketball.

5. Is anybody on the bus missing their jacket?

6. She wants to know who's exhibit has won the prize.

7. Either I or my cousin will complete the contract.

8. Mrs. Rossi remembered more of the movie than her.

9. In the playoffs next week, us loyal fans will be cheering every minute.

10. Are you as happy as I?

11. The company wrote to my friend and I about our guarantees.

12. If someone plans to volunteer, you should give Carlos your name.

Part Two Correct any pronoun errors that you find in the following letter. Apply the rules of formal English usage.

Dear Mrs. Lasky:

I hope this note will explain my absences last week.

On Monday, my brother and me had to take my sister Angie to the hospital. Somebody had left their skateboard on the steps, and she tripped on it.

On Wednesday, us track team members were asked to report one hour early. Its not going to happen again. The coach wanted everyone to be measured for their uniform. (Just between you and me, the uniforms have too much purple on the top. But the players chose the colors themselfs.)

On Friday, my Mom asked my brother and myself to bring Angie home. If someone wants to leave that hospital, you should have cash for your bill because its not easy to get a check approved. No one should need to wait two hours to pay her bill. I hope your going to excuse these three absences.

Thank you,

Joe Williams

Capitalization, Placement of Modifiers, Parallel Structure, and Irregular Verbs

20 Capitalization

The general principle behind capitalization is that **proper nouns** (names of *specific* persons, places, or things) are capitalized. **Common nouns** (names of *general* persons, places, or things) are *not* capitalized.

Study the following sentences, each of which illustrates a rule of capitalization.

1. Capitalize all parts of a person's name.

Many children are familiar with the poetry and novels of *Robert Louis Stevenson.*

2. Capitalize the titles of relatives only when the titles precede the person's name or when they take the place of a person's name.

My *U*ncle Clarence is a carpenter.
Happy birthday, *M*other.
       but
My *u*ncle and my *m*other are both retired.

The same rule applies to professional titles.

I saw *Dr.* Walsh today.
> but

Only a *d*octor can perform surgery.

3. Capitalize the names of streets, cities, and states.

My brother lives at 194 *M*idland *A*venue, *O*maha, *N*ebraska.

4. Capitalize the names of countries, languages, and ethnic groups.

Most of the people in *C*anada speak *E*nglish, but many *C*anadians also speak *F*rench.

5. Capitalize the names of specific buildings, geographical features, schools, and other institutions.

Our tour of the city included *D*avies *S*ymphony *H*all, *N*ob *H*ill, *G*olden *G*ate *P*ark, the *U*niversity of *S*an *F*rancisco, and the *N*ational *M*aritime *M*useum.

6. Capitalize the days of the week, the months of the year, and the names of holidays. Do *not* capitalize the names of the seasons of the year.

We usually celebrate *T*hanksgiving on the last *T*hursday in *N*ovember.
I like to see the leaves change color in *a*utumn.

7. Capitalize directions of the compass only when they refer to specific regions.

The population of the United States is shifting away from the *N*ortheast toward the *S*outh and the *S*outhwest.

8. Capitalize the names of companies and brand names but not the names of the products themselves.

*P*roctor & *G*amble manufactures *I*vory *S*oap.
Have you ever eaten a *H*ershey *c*hocolate *b*ar?

9. Capitalize the first word of every sentence.

10. Capitalize the subject pronoun *I*.

11. Capitalize the first word of a title and all other words in the title except for articles *(a, an, the)* and except for conjunctions and prepositions that have fewer than five letters.

   John Steinbeck wrote *The Grapes of Wrath* and *Of Mice and Men*.

12. Capitalize the names of academic subjects only if they are already proper nouns or if they are common nouns followed by a course number.

   This semester I am taking *E*nglish, *c*hemistry, and *P*sychology 101.

13. Capitalize the names of specific historical events, such as wars, revolutions, religious and political movements, and specific eras.

   The *H*undred *Y*ears' *W*ar was fought between England and France from 1337 to 1453.
   Martin Luther was a key figure in the *P*rotestant *R*eformation.
   The *R*oaring *T*wenties came to an end with the start of the *D*epression.

EXERCISE 20A

Add capital letters to the following sentences wherever they are necessary.

1. The camel, an animal native to asia, is rarely seen in the united states except in zoos or circuses.

2. But a cousin of the camel, the south american llama, is becoming a familiar sight to americans of the far west, especially to those who hike in the rockies or sierras.

3. The llama, which looks like a small hairy camel without a hump, is the main domesticated animal of the indians who live high in the andes mountains of south america.

4. For them it not only supplies meat, milk, and wool, but it also packs loads on the high and treacherous andean trails.

5. It is mainly as pack animals that llamas are being bred and trained in the western united states.

6. Llamas can carry up to eighty pounds each, yet they do almost no damage to trails, which makes the u.s. forest service happy.

7. They need little water or food while on the trail, and they are generally gentle and easily trained.

8. Trained llamas and guides are now available for hikers in colorado, utah, montana, oregon, and california.

9. Llamas are in short supply because the u.s. customs bureau now prohibits their importation for fear of hoof and mouth disease.

10. Even though a young female llama may cost more than four thousand dollars, the american llama breeders' association is growing rapidly as more people are attracted to this most useful and most intriguing animal.

EXERCISE 20B

Add capital letters to the following sentences wherever they are necessary.

1. does george know that we're going to the dress rehearsal for the musical *oklahoma* on wednesday?

2. marie wanted to take chemistry 101, but professor wilson convinced her to take a mathematics course first.

3. she never buys any brand but chicken of the sea tuna, which is a product of the ralston purina company.

4. when margaret mitchell, an unknown novelist from atlanta, georgia, sat down to write an epic novel about the civil war, she never dreamed that her book *gone with the wind* would become an all-time best seller, would be made into an academy award-winning motion picture, and would bring her a pulitzer prize.

5. did you tell grandfather that his doctor is on vacation and that he is supposed to see dr. jones instead?

6. she speaks french and italian, but she has never been to france or italy.

7. not all revolutions have been as successful as the american revolution.

8. she likes most cola drinks, but pepsi is her favorite.

9. he forgot to give her a valentine on valentine's day, so she gave him a book called *you and your memory* for april fool's day.

EXERCISE 20C

Some capitalization rules include exceptions to the rule. For each of the rules listed below, write one sentence of your own that illustrates both the rule *and* its exception.

1. The rule about the names of academic subjects:

_____

_____

2. The rule about directions of the compass:

_____

_____

3. The rule about the titles of relatives:

_____

_____

4. The rule about words in the title of a book, movie, television program, etc.:

_____

_____

5. The rule about companies and brand names:

_____

_____

6. The rule about periods of time, such as days of the week, months of the year:

_____

_____

7. The rule about professional titles:

_____

_____

21 Misplaced and Dangling Modifiers

Modifiers are words that are used to describe other words in a sentence. A modifier may be a single word, a phrase, or a clause. (Adjective clauses are discussed in Lesson 14.) Examples of some of the more common types of modifiers are given below. Circle the word that each italicized modifier describes.

ADJECTIVE The bride wore a *white* dress.

ADJECTIVE CLAUSE The man *who is following you* is a private investigator.

PREPOSITIONAL PHRASE The car *in the driveway* is mine.

The words you should have circled are *dress,* which is modified by ''white,'' *man,* which is modified by ''who is following you,'' and *car,* which is modified by ''in the driveway.''

Another type of modifier is a **participial phrase.** A participial phrase begins with a participle. A **participle** is a verb form that functions as an adjective. There are two kinds of participles. **Present participles** are formed by adding *-ing* to the main verb (for example, *walking, knowing, seeing*.) **Past participles** are the verb forms that are used with the helping verb *have* (have *walked,* have *known,* have *seen*). Circle the word that each of the following participial phrases modifies.

Hoping to win a prize, I entered my name in the contest.

The chocolate candy *made by this company* is famous all over the world.

The words that you should have circled are *I* and *candy.*

If you look back at all the words that you have circled so far in this lesson, you will notice that although modifiers sometimes precede and sometimes follow the words they describe, they are in all cases placed as close as possible to the word that they describe. Failure to place a modifier in the correct position in a sentence results in an error known as a **misplaced modifier.**

MISPLACED John told a story to his friend *with a surprise ending.*
(Does John's friend have a surprise ending?)
CORRECT John told a story *with a surprise ending* to his friend.
MISPLACED Harry gave flowers to his wife *purchased at the supermarket.*
(Was Harry's wife purchased at the supermarket?)
CORRECT Harry gave flowers *purchased at the supermarket* to his wife.

Correct the misplaced modifiers in the following sentences.

The mother gave cookies to her children taken fresh from the oven.

Elaine bought a dress at a small shop that was on sale for twenty dollars.

The host served spareribs to his hungry guests basted with barbeque sauce.

The teacher wrote sentences that squeaked on the blackboard with chalk.

Another kind of misplaced modifier involves the incorrect placement of correlative conjunctions. **Correlative conjunctions** are conjunctions that occur in pairs, such as:

both . . . and
either . . . or
neither . . . nor
not only . . . but also

Since these conjunctions occur in pairs, they are usually used to compare two ideas. For example:

The refugees had *neither* food *nor* shelter.

The rule for using correlative conjunctions is that the conjunctions *must be placed as close as possible to the words that are being compared.* For example:

I will major in *either* art *or* music.
                    not
I *either* will major in art *or* music.

Study the following examples of correctly and incorrectly placed correlative conjunctions.

INCORRECT   You *not only* need to see a doctor *but also* a lawyer.
CORRECT   You need to see *not only* a doctor *but also* a lawyer.
INCORRECT   She *both* speaks French *and* Italian.
CORRECT   She speaks *both* French *and* Italian.

Correct the misplaced correlative conjunctions in the following sentences.

Neither he reads nor writes English.

Your new car both is attractive and economical.

They not only have vacationed in Hawaii but also in Tahiti.

You either must work fewer hours or take fewer classes.

An error related to the misplaced modifier is the **dangling modifier.** A dangling modifier sometimes occurs when a participial phrase is placed at the beginning of a sentence. A participial phrase in this position *must describe the subject of the following clause.* If the subject of the clause cannot logically perform the action described in the participial phrase, the phrase is said to "dangle" (to hang loosely, without a logical connection).

DANGLING   *After getting married,* Marsha's problems increased.
           (This sentence suggests that Marsha's *problems* got married.)
CORRECT   After *Marsha* got married, her problems increased.

DANGLING   *While making breakfast,* my bacon burned.

(This sentence suggests that my *bacon* was making breakfast.)

CORRECT   While *I* was making breakfast, my bacon burned.

or

While making breakfast, I burned my bacon.

(Use a comma after a participial phrase at the beginning of a sentence.)

Notice that there are several ways to correct dangling modifiers. You may add a noun or pronoun to the sentence to provide a word that the modifier can logically describe, or you may reword the entire sentence. *However, simply reversing the order of the dangling modifier and the rest of the sentence does not correct the error.*

DANGLING   *While cooking,* her smoke alarm went off.

STILL DANGLING   Her smoke alarm went off *while cooking.*

CORRECT   While *she* was cooking, her smoke alarm went off.

Revise the following sentences so that they no longer contain dangling modifiers.

While doing his homework, the phone rang.

Hoping for a raise, her work improved.

While waiting for the bus, my feet began to hurt.

Knowing all the answers, the test was easy.

Because misplaced and dangling modifiers create confusing and even absurd sentences, you should be careful to avoid them in your writing.

EXERCISE 21A

Part One Construct five sentences of your own, using the modifiers listed below at the beginning of your sentences. Make certain that your modifiers do not dangle.

1. By leaving before sunrise, _____

_____

2. In order to increase sales, _____

_____

3. While listening to the new record, _____

_____

4. After eating nine pancakes, _____

_____

5. Not seeing the car in the fog, _____

_____

Part Two Rewrite each of the following sentences so that none contains a dangling or misplaced modifier.

6. Coming around the corner, the Golden Gate Bridge became visible.

_____

_____

7. She sent a package to her aunt that contained six quarts of whiskey.

_____

_____

8. While running for a touchdown, his shoe came off.

_____

_____

9. She always ate cereal with a certain expression that was sweetened by honey.

_____

_____

10. To win at this game, the rules must be thoroughly understood.

_____

_____

life prisoner,
Capital punishment
Abortion
Anti-abortion.

EXERCISE 21B

Some of the following sentences contain misplaced modifiers, dangling modifiers, or incorrectly placed correlative conjunctions. Rewrite these sentences. If a sentence is correctly constructed, label it *C* for *correct*.

1. While fixing the salad, my cake burned in the oven. *(handwritten: it was)*

   (handwritten: or, I burned my cake . . .)

2. I either must borrow some money or reduce my spending.

3. He sent fifty dollars to the girl that he won in a poker game.

   (handwritten: He sent the girl $50 he won in a poker game)

4. Knowing that she would always be welcome, Marita returned for a short visit. *(handwritten: C)*

5. To become a supervisor, Ella not only passed a written exam but she underwent also a series of interviews.

6. He found the broken part seeing a crack in the fitting.

_____

_____

7. He was both strong enough to overpower his opponents and smart enough to outthink them.

_____

_____

8. They not only rarely disagree but also wisely settle differences quickly.

_____

_____

9. To win her approval, your behavior must be gentlemanly.

_____

_____

10. Some of his favorite songs are heard while listening to the radio.

_____

_____

EXERCISE 21C

Some of the following sentences contain misplaced modifiers, dangling modifiers, or incorrectly placed correlative conjunctions. Rewrite these sentences. If a sentence is correctly constructed, label it *C* for *correct*.

1. While typing the letter, my typewriter broke.

   _____

   _____

2. I used a bottle of pills that had been prescribed for my sister.

   _____

   _____

3. For winning the prize, her father was proud of her.

   _____

   _____

4. His understanding of algebra improved after taking Ms. Ramirez for the course.

   _____

   _____

5. They neither are good friends nor good neighbors.

   _____

   _____

6. They played songs for the visitors that had not been heard in many years.

_____

_____

7. Hoping to score more points, her technique was modified.

_____

_____

8. Seeing the doctor periodically, she kept track of her hearing disorder.

_____

_____

9. To increase its flavor, chilis should go in the sauce.

_____

_____

10. The photograph portrayed a puppy chewing a bone with curly black hair.

_____

_____

22 Parallel Structure

The term **parallel structure** means that similar ideas should be expressed in similar grammatical structures. For example, Benjamin Franklin quoted the following proverb:

Early to bed and early to rise make a man healthy, wealthy, and wise.

This proverb is a good illustration of parallel structure. It begins with two similar phrases, "early to bed" and "early to rise," and it ends with a series of three similar words (they are all adjectives): *healthy, wealthy,* and *wise*.

In contrast, the following two versions of the same proverb contain some words that are *not* parallel.

Early to bed and early *rising* make a man healthy, wealthy, and wise.
Early to bed and early to rise make a man healthy, wealthy, and *give wisdom*.

Therefore, these last two sentences are *not* properly constructed.

Since there are many different grammatical structures in the English language, the possibilities for constructing non-parallel sentences may appear to be almost unlimited. Fortunately, you do not have to be able to identify all the grammatical structures in a sentence in order to tell whether or not that sentence has parallel structure. Sentences that lack parallel structure are usually so awkward that they are easy to recognize.

NOT PARALLEL   I enjoy *swimming, surfing,* and *to sail.*
PARALLEL   I enjoy *swimming, surfing,* and *sailing.*
NOT PARALLEL   The doctor told me *to stay* in bed, *that I should drink* lots of liquids, and *to take* two aspirins every four hours.
PARALLEL   The doctor told me *to stay* in bed, *to drink* lots of liquids, and *to take* two aspirins every four hours.
NOT PARALLEL   He wrote *quickly, carefully,* and *with clarity.*
PARALLEL   He wrote *quickly, carefully,* and *clearly.*

Revise each of the following sentences so that it is parallel in structure.

Potatoes can be boiled, baked, or you can fry them.

The movie was a success because of its good acting, interesting plot, and its special effects were exciting.

Please list your name, how old you are, and your birthplace.

The Admissions Office told me to read the college catalog and that I should make an appointment with a counselor.

EXERCISE 22A

Rewrite any sentences that lack parallel structure. If a sentence is already parallel, label it *C* for *correct*.

1. Marsha was tall, athletic, and had brown eyes.

_____

_____

2. He likes to swim and playing handball.

_____

_____

3. They go to visit relatives every summer or stay here in Springville.

_____

_____

4. You can wash the dishes or mop the floor.

_____

_____

5. The message was confusing, insulting, and in poor taste.

_____

_____

6. Turn out the lights, close up your shop, and go to the concert with me.

_____

_____

7. They asked us for our license and to sit still.

_____

_____

8. The girls will soon be here and will know the answer.

_____

_____

9. Tell Charley how to get there and that he is to bring the hot dogs.

_____

_____

10. She makes tacos that are full of good meat, topped with cheese and salsa, and have just the right combination of flavors.

_____

_____

EXERCISE 22B

Rewrite any sentences that lack parallel structure. If a sentence is already parallel, label it *C* for *correct*.

1. Rosa was friendly, intelligent, and had good manners.

_____

_____

2. Wilson worked hard, played hard, and acted hard.

_____

_____

3. The boss asked Lena to fix the machine and be faster.

_____

_____

4. Use fresh vegetables and sour cream that is fresh.

_____

_____

5. That course emphasizes how to use a microscope and cell structure.

_____

_____

6. Be there on time and on your best behavior.

_____

_____

7. Johnson stole the ball, dribbled it downcourt, and made the winning basket!

_____

_____

8. Here are your instructions, and there is the equipment.

_____

_____

9. Go with George, stay with George, and leave with George.

_____

_____

10. Mexico has beautiful tropical beaches, lush productive farmlands, and cities that are overcrowded.

_____

_____

23 Irregular Verbs

Verbs have three **principal** (meaning ''most important'') **parts:** the *present* (which, when preceded by *to,* becomes the *infinitive*), the *past,* and the *past participle*.

The **present** form may stand alone as a main verb without any helping verb. For example:

I *live* in California.
Many students *ride* the bus to school.

It may also be preceded by a helping verb, such as *can, could, do, does, did, may, might, must, shall, should, will,* or *would.* (A list of helping verbs appears in Lesson 4, p. 38.)

John *should see* a doctor.
She *may need* a new car.

However, the present form is *not* used after any forms of the helping verbs *have (has, have, had)* or *be (am, is, are, was, were, been)*.

The **past** form is used alone as a main verb. It is *not* preceded by a helping verb.

Our friends *left* town yesterday.
The class *began* twenty minutes ago.

The **past participle** is *always* preceded by at least one, and sometimes more than one, helping verb. The helping verb is often a form of *have* or *be*.

I *have washed* the car.
The vegetables *were grown* in our garden.

Most English verbs are regular. A **regular** verb forms both its past and past participle by adding *-ed* to the present. (If the present already ends in *-e,* only a *-d* is added.)

Present	*Past*	*Past Participle*
talk	talked	talked
like	liked	liked

Notice that with regular verbs, the past and the past participle are spelled the same.

Any verb that does *not* form both its past and past participle by adding *-ed* or *-d* is considered **irregular.** For example:

Present	*Past*	*Past Participle*
eat	ate	eaten
write	wrote	written
begin	began	begun

Since irregular verbs by definition have irregular spellings, you must *memorize* the spelling of their past and past participle forms. Irregular verbs include many of the most commonly used verbs in the English language (for example, *come, go, eat, drink, sit, stand*), so it is important to study them carefully.

Here is a list of some of the most commonly used irregular verbs. In addition to learning the verbs on this list, if you are not sure whether or not a verb is irregular, look it up in the dictionary. A good dictionary will list the principal parts of an irregular verb in addition to defining its meaning.

Present	Past	Past Participle
beat	beat	beaten
begin	began	begun
bend	bent	bent
bleed	bled	bled
blow	blew	blown
break	broke	broken
bring	brought	brought
build	built	built
buy	bought	bought
catch	caught	caught
choose	chose	chosen
come	came	come
cut	cut	cut
do	did	done
draw	drew	drawn
drink	drank	drunk
drive	drove	driven
eat	ate	eaten
fall	fell	fallen
feed	fed	fed
feel	felt	felt
find	found	found
fly	flew	flown
freeze	froze	frozen
get	got	got *or* gotten
give	gave	given
go	went	gone
grow	grew	grown
have	had	had
hear	heard	heard
hide	hid	hidden
hit	hit	hit
hurt	hurt	hurt
keep	kept	kept
know	knew	known
lay	laid	laid
leave	left	left
lend	lent	lent
lie	lay	lain
lose	lost	lost
make	made	made
mean	meant	meant
meet	met	met
pay	paid	paid
put	put	put
read	read	read
ride	rode	ridden
ring	rang	rung
rise	rose	risen
run	ran	run
see	saw	seen
sell	sold	sold
send	sent	sent
set	set	set
shake	shook	shaken
shoot	shot	shot
sing	sang	sung
sink	sank	sunk
sit	sat	sat
sleep	slept	slept
speak	spoke	spoken
spend	spent	spent
spin	spun	spun
stand	stood	stood
steal	stole	stolen
stick	stuck	stuck
swear	swore	sworn
swim	swam	swum
take	took	taken
tear	tore	torn
tell	told	told
think	thought	thought
throw	threw	thrown
wear	wore	worn
weep	wept	wept
win	won	won
write	wrote	written

Notice that compound verbs follow the same pattern as their root forms. For example:

be*come*	be*came*	be*come*
for*give*	for*gave*	for*given*
under*stand*	under*stood*	under*stood*

EXERCISE 23A

Circle the verb form that correctly completes each sentence. If you are not absolutely certain of the correct form, go back to the list of irregular verbs *before* you make your choice.

1. She (winned, won) the race.

2. Roger has (went, gone) to boot camp.

3. She (payed, paid) $16.50 for the shoes.

4. Her uncle had (drawn, drawed) her portrait.

5. They must have (drank, drunk) all the water.

6. Monica's sister just (lays, lies) on the couch all day.

7. The weeds (grew, growed) back in the flower bed.

8. He has (flew, flown) almost every type of airplane.

9. They (chose, choosed) a new captain.

10. That Ford has (sat, set) there for over a week.

11. She has (rose, risen) promptly at sunrise all summer.

12. Frank (builded, built) a new patio last summer.

13. The company has always (sworn, swore) by its products.

14. They have (became, become) good friends.

15. That chicken (layed, laid) the most eggs.

16. Her children have (driven, drove) her crazy.

17. John's relatives (was, were) all from Chicago.

18. I think Angel (eat, ate) too much pie.

19. George has (rode, ridden) the same horse every year.

20. The ice has (freezed, frozen) solid.

21. Has she (done, did) all her homework?

22. Have the replacement parts for the motor (come, came) yet?

23. The neighbors (brung, brought) their son to school.

24. Last week he (ran, run) his fastest race.

25. Has Roger ever (sang, sung) that song before?

26. Irene (swum, swam) the length of the pool.

EXERCISE 23B

For each of the following irregular verbs show the correct *past* and *past participle* forms. Then construct two sentences that use those forms. The first verb has been done as an example.

1. choose: _____*chose*_____   _____*chosen*_____

_____*Richard chose the largest banana.*_____

_____*They have chosen Lori as their leader.*_____

2. grow: _____   _____

_____

_____

3. read: _____   _____

_____

_____

4. set: _____   _____

_____

_____

5. lie ("to recline"): _____   _____

_____

_____

6. sink: _____   _____

_____

_____

7. throw: _____   _____

_____

_____

8. sleep: _____   _____

_____

_____

9. lend: _____   _____

_____

_____

10. come: _____   _____

_____

_____

11. rise: _____   _____

_____

_____

12. get: _____   _____

_____

_____

13. know: _____   _____

_____

_____

Capitalization,
Placement of Modifiers,
Parallel Structure, and Irregular Verbs
Unit Review

Part One Add capital letters to the following passage wherever they are needed.

on november 19, 1977, station wnet/channel 13 showed an hour-long documentary honoring a ninety-year-old woman artist. that woman is still alive and still painting in her middle nineties. she lives in abiquiu, new mexico, and her name is georgia o'keeffe.

georgia o'keeffe was born on the 19th of november in 1887. after growing up on a farm in wisconsin, she studied commercial art at the art institute of chicago. she switched to teaching art for a few years on the advice of alon bement, one of her summer teachers at the university of virginia in charlottesville. she loved her teaching years in what she called "the wild west" of amarillo, texas. in 1916 the noted photographer alfred stieglitz put some of o'keeffe's drawings on display in new york. since then she has had continuing success as a painter.

one of her early favorite subjects was flowers, which she painted on huge canvasses. *black iris,* painted in 1926, now hangs in new york's metropolitan museum of art. o'keeffe and stieglitz, who became her husband, painted and photographed many parts of the u.s. in succeeding years. she liked to climb in her old ford and roam wherever she wished until she had a car full of finished pictures.

new mexico became her favorite subject and eventually her home. she has lived there and continues to paint there ever since stieglitz died. o'keeffe was the first woman artist to be awarded america's presidential medal of freedom.

Part Two Some of the following sentences contain misplaced or dangling modifiers; others lack parallel structure. Rewrite these incorrect sentences. If a sentence contains no structural errors, label it *C* for *correct*.

1. To pass Physics 101, your test scores must average 70 percent or higher.

_____

_____

2. The Spanish proverb *Llegar y besar* ("To arrive and to kiss") is usually translated as "No sooner said than done."

_____

_____

3. To do well at spearfishing, use the correct type of spear, the right size of swimfins, and have a mask that fits.

_____

_____

4. After her bridal shower, she had not only a good start on a trousseau but also a large number of household items.

_____

_____

5. Hoping his opponent would not notice, his tactics became more subtle.

_____

_____

6. By taking a shortcut, the distance to Des Moines was reduced by a third.

_____

_____

7. We looked forward to a big dinner with our friends with spaghetti.

_____

_____

Part Three   Correct any improper verb forms in the following paragraphs.

Ginny was laying near the edge of the pool. The sun had rose high in the sky, and her sunburn had become worse. Tony told her, "If you lie there much longer, you will look like a crab that has been throwed in boiling water!"

"I have ran completely out of suntan lotion; I told Jerry he should have brought an extra bottle. After you have went to the Post Office, Tony, will you take a minute to get some more? And don't forget to return the book that Rosie loaned me last week. She hasn't forgave me for losing her cigarette lighter.

"I'll get the lotion, Ginny, but you'll have to see Rosie. I could have swore it was she who mislaid the lighter. I have told her so, but her opinion can't be shook once she makes up her mind."

Index

```
          4
          5
          6
        E 7
        F 8
        G 9
        H 0
        I 1
        J 2
```